T0199116

LOVE, CARE, AND PATRIOTISM

An Essay Guide to Raising Good Citizens

LINDA MKRTCHYAN, MA

iUniverse

LOVE, CARE, AND PATRIOTISM
AN ESSAY GUIDE TO RAISING GOOD CITIZENS

iUniverse books may be ordered through booksellers or by contacting:

iUniverse
1663 Liberty Drive
Bloomington, IN 47403
www.iuniverse.com
1-800-Authors (1-800-288-4677)

Because of the dynamic nature of the internet, any web addresses or links contained in this book may have changed since publication and may no longer be valid. The views expressed in this work are solely those of the author and do not necessarily reflect the views of the publisher, and the publisher hereby disclaims any responsibility for them.

Any people depicted in stock imagery provided by Getty Images are models, and such images are being used for illustrative purposes only.
Certain stock imagery © Getty Images.

ISBN: 978-1-5320-5999-5 (sc)
ISBN: 978-1-5320-6001-4 (hc)
ISBN: 978-1-5320-6000-7 (e)

Library of Congress Control Number: 2018912537

Print information available on the last page.

iUniverse rev. date: 11/29/2018

While assigning the discussions, sentences, paragraphs, or essays, the teacher's job will be to explain some of the appropriate ways for the students to express themselves that fit within the educational norm. This book is for conversations and topics for discussions, writing few sentences, paragraphs, or essays.

FOR FIRST-GRADE STUDENTS

The topics for this age are for conversation only. The teacher's job will be to explain some of the appropriate ways for students to express themselves that fit within the educational norm.

My Birthday

Think about three things that changed after your birthday, and talk about them. See whether the following items apply:

> You got a new thing for your birthday.
> This year you are choosing to have a better lifestyle.
> You are going to try something new.
> The new good thing you want to do at this age is …
> Some of the fun summer activities this year for you are going to be …

I Am …

Think about three things you like, and talk about them. See whether the following items apply:

> what you do every day
> your reliability
> friends
> family
> the things you want
> the things you need
> putting your seat belt on
> doing good
> helping
> cleaning
> taking care of your things
> a birthday gift
> your toys
> books
> your siblings

home
your country

I Am Grateful for ...

Think about three things you are grateful for, and talk about them.
See whether the following items apply:

    your family
    your country
    your looks
    your belongings
    your habits
    your friends
    your neighborhood
    your opportunities
    your school
    your classmates
    your cousins
    your siblings
    your health
    your happiness
    holidays
    summer vacation

Education is...

Think about three things that you agree with or know about education
and talk about them. See whether the following items apply:

    It is easier to become a Doctor than to become a millionaire
    It is easier to make money, when you are a Doctor
    Education helps become more knowledgeable
    Education helps boost self-esteem
    Education is fun, if you are interested in it
    Education is a brain exercise

Education helps solve problems easier
Education can help earn respect
Education makes it easier to buy a lot of things you want
With education you can have your own business
Education is a prestige
Once you become a Doctor, you will be a Doctor for the rest of your life
Education does not make you boring
Education can give you more than what money can
With education you can have money
With education you can have a stable job by the time you are a middle aged person.
To become educated all you have to do is pick a subject and do your homework
Many people can help you become educated
To become a Doctor all you need to do is continue your education and do your homework
With education you may never become homeless
You can be educated as well as an entrepreneur
You can be educated as well as a millionaire
It is very easy to become educated if you have a favorite subject
Your favorite subject in school is...
Your feelings about educated people are

I Feel Smart and/or Strong When ...

Think of three things you do that make you feel smart and/or strong, and talk about them. See whether the following items apply:

getting good grades
learning new words
choosing better vocabulary
when doing homework
when finishing homework
when friends call
when playing outdoors

when parents say you did a good job
when exercising
when it's a birthday
when thinking about good things
when putting the dishes in the sink

Growing Up

Think of three things about growing up, and talk about them. See whether the following items apply:

What is being a grown-up?
Are you a grown-up yet?
Name some of the things grown-ups do for themselves.
Name some of the things grown-ups do for family.
Name some of the things grown-ups do for relatives (hint: saying nice things).
Name some of the things grown-ups do for friends.
Name some of the things grown-ups do for your country.

My Culture ...

Think of three things you love about your culture, and talk about them. See whether the following items apply:

movies
music
your cultural values
your cultural rituals
food
presidents
entertainers
talk shows
radio shows
compare old movies and songs to new movies and songs
cartoons

fun community activities

museums

Good Person

Think of three things about any good person you know, and talk about them. See whether the following items apply:

is whom you approve of as a good person

is whom Mom and Dad do not disapprove of

is kind

is helpful

is considerate

is responsible

does not harm others

does not let others hurt himself or herself

sets good examples

is nice to pets

waters the plants

is caring

is grateful

can say nice things

Love Is ...

Think of three things you love, and talk about them. See whether the following items apply:

love for family

love for friends

love for exercise

love for fun

love for country

love for entertainment

love for nature

love for classmates

love for school
love for food
love for respect
love for attention
reading fairy tales
bringing flowers

Being a Hero Is When I Am ...

Think of three things that make you feel like a hero, and talk about them. See whether the following items apply:

not peeing in bed
acting friendly
tying your shoes
choosing good words
not throwing tantrums but talking instead
being on time to school
being responsible for yourself
not forgetting fun
considering the cost and benefits for your actions
knowing what's good for you

I Am a Good Child for My Family

Think of three good things you and your family members do for one another, and talk about them. See whether the following items apply:

having loving parents
having caring parents
doing laundry
having a warm bed
having shoes that fit
washing dishes
making food

having clothing
having a roof over your head
others listening to you sing
others playing sports with you
your parents putting your picture on the fridge
getting gifts
giving gifts
making your bed
saying thank you
putting the dishes into the sink
helping with homework
putting your shoes where they are supposed to be
respecting the elderly

Self-Control Is When I Am ...

Think of three things you have self-control in, and talk about them.
See whether the following items apply:

not taking cookies from cookie jars
doing your homework on time
not talking loudly in the classroom
dressing up appropriately
keeping cell phones on mute and controlling your phone
(instead of your phone controlling you)
using your words and not screaming
not arguing but saying please
not eating too many holiday candies

I Am Responsible When I Am ...

Think of three responsibilities, and talk about them. See whether
the following items apply:

doing your homework on time
eating healthy food

putting dishes into the sink after dinner
putting shoes in the closet
not losing things

I Am Having Fun When I Am ...

Think of three fun things, and talk about them. See whether the
following items apply:

playing sports
camping
jumping
running
going to a birthday
playing with pets
playing board games
watching games
dancing
swimming
making new friends
visiting grandparents
meeting with relatives
traveling throughout the United States

Girls Are Similar to and Different from Boys ...

Think of three things about girls and boys that are similar or
different, and talk about them. See whether the following items
apply:

choice of clothing
shoes
interests
hobbies
games
dream job

food
exercise habits
sport activities
hair color
eye color
cars they drive
last names
signing abilities
dancing abilities
abilities to do school work
abilities to put their shoes in their proper place
abilities for washing the dishes

Me and My Country

Think of three things you love about your country, and talk about them. See whether the following items apply:

celebrating national holidays
watching fireworks
buying American products
watching American movies
celebrating New Year
celebrating Martin Luther King Jr. Day
celebrating George Washington's birthday
Memorial Day
celebrating Independence Day
celebrating Labor Day
celebrating Columbus Day
celebrating Veterans Day
celebrating Thanksgiving Day
celebrating Christmas Day
enjoying American entertainments
knowing who our president is
keeping our American traditions

FOR
SECOND-GRADE
STUDENTS

My Birthday

Think of three things about your birthday, and talk about them. See whether the following items apply:

> a new thing you got for your birthday
> this year you are choosing to do something new
> the new good thing you want to do at this age is ...
> some of the fun summer activities for you this year will be ...

I Am ...

Think of three good things about yourself, and talk about them. See whether the following items apply:

> What is your day like?
> friends
> wanting something
> needing something
> putting your seat belt on
> doing good
> helping
> cleaning
> taking care of your things
> your birthday gifts
> your toys
> books
> siblings
> home
> country

I Am Grateful for …

Think about three things you are grateful for, and talk about them. See whether the following items apply:

> your family
> your country
> your looks
> your belongings
> your habits
> your friends
> your neighborhood
> your opportunities
> your school
> your classmates
> your cousins
> your siblings
> your health
> your happiness
> holidays
> summer vacation

Education is…

Think about three things that you agree with or know about education and talk about them. See whether the following items apply:

> It is easier to become a Doctor than to become a millionaire
> It is easier to make money, when you are a Doctor
> Education helps become more knowledgeable
> Education helps boost self-esteem
> Education is fun, if you are interested in it
> Education is a brain exercise
> Education helps solve problems easier
> Education can help earn respect
> Education makes it easier to buy a lot of things you want
> With education you can have your own business

Education is a prestige

Once you become a Doctor, you will be a Doctor for the rest of your life

Education does not make you boring

Education can give you more than what money can

With education you can have money

With education you can have a stable job by the time you are a middle aged person.

To become educated all you have to do is pick a subject and do your homework

Many people can help you become educated

To become a Doctor all you need to do is continue your education and do your homework

With education you may never become homeless

You can be educated as well as an entrepreneur

You can be educated as well as a millionaire

It is very easy to become educated if you have a favorite subject

Your favorite subject in school is...

Your feelings about educated people are

I Feel Smart and/or Strong When ...

Think of three things you do that make you feel smart and/or strong, and talk about them. See whether the following items apply:

when you get good grades
when you learn new words
when you use clean words
when doing homework
when finishing homework
when exercising
when friends call
when playing outdoors
when your parents say you have done a good job
when it's your birthday
when you think about good things

when you put your dishes in the sink

My Culture ...

Think of three things you love about your culture, and talk about them. See whether the following items apply:

>   values
>   rituals
>   movies
>   music
>   food
>   presidents
>   entertainers
>   talk shows
>   radio shows
>   compare old movies and songs to new movies and songs
>   cartoons
>   fun community activities
>   camping
>   museums

I Am a Good Child for My Family

Think of three good things that you and your family members do for one another, and talk about them. See whether the following items apply:

>   being grateful for having a loving family
>   having caring parents
>   doing laundry
>   having a warm bed
>   having shoes that fit
>   washing dishes
>   having food
>   having clothes

having a roof over your head
others listening to you sing
others listening to you reading
others playing sports with you
your parents putting your picture on the fridge
getting gifts
giving gifts
making your bed
saying thank you
cleaning the table
helping with homework
putting your shoes where they are supposed to be
showing respect to the elderly

Being a Hero Is When I Am ...

Think of three things that make you feel like a hero, and talk about
them. See whether the following items apply:

acting friendly
using clean words
being on time to school
being responsible for yourself
having fun
knowing what's good for you

The Support System in My Life ...

Think of three things you like about your family and friends, and
talk about them. See whether the following items apply:

socializing with your mom
socializing with your dad
socializing with your sister
socializing with your brother
socializing with your aunts

socializing with your uncles
socializing with your cousins
socializing with your friends
socializing with your old neighbors
socializing with your new neighbors
socializing with your family friends
socializing with your friends at school
socializing with your classmates
socializing with your teachers
socializing with your mom's friends' children
socializing with your dad's friends' children

Self-Control Is When I Am ...

Think of three things you have self-control in, and talk about them.
See whether the following items apply:

not taking cookies from cookie jars
participating in the classroom instead of talking
exercising
dressing up appropriately
using your words and not screaming
keeping your cell phone on mute and controlling your phone
(instead of your phone controlling you)
not eating too many holiday candies
putting away your shoes
not interrupting
not talking during class

I Am Responsible When I Am ...

Think of three things that you are responsible for, and talk about
them. See whether the following items apply:

doing your homework on time
eating healthy food

cleaning the table
putting your shoes in the closet
tying your shoes when you are wearing them
not losing things
asking your parents whether you are a responsible child

I Am Having Fun When I Am ...

Think of three fun things, and talk about them. See whether the following items apply:

playing sports
camping
playing board games
playing with pets
watching games
dancing
making friends
talking to friends
swimming
meeting with relatives
traveling throughout the United States

Girls Are Similar to and Different from Boys ...

Think of three things about girls and boys that are similar or different, and talk about them. See whether the following items apply:

choice of clothing
shoes
interests
hobbies
games
dream job
food

exercise habits
sport activities
hair color
eye color
cars they drive
last names
signing abilities
dancing abilities
abilities to do school work
abilities to put their shoes in their proper place

Growing Up

Think of three things about growing up, and talk about them. See whether the following items apply:

What are grown-ups like?
Are you a grown-up yet?
What are some of the things grown-ups do for themselves?
What are some of the things grown-ups do for their family?
What are some of the things grown-ups do for their relatives (hint: saying nice things)?
What are some of the things grown-ups do for their friends?
What are some of the things grown-ups do for your country?

Good Person

Think of three things you like about anyone you find is a good person, and talk about them. See whether the following items apply:

is whom you approve of as a good person
is whom Mom and Dad do not disapprove of
is kind
is helpful
is considerate
is responsible

does not harm others
does not let others hurt himself or herself
sets good examples
is nice to pets
waters the plants
is caring
is grateful
can say nice things

Love Is ...

Think of three things you love, and talk about them. See whether the following items apply:

love for family
love for friends
love for exercise
love for fun
love for country
love for entertainment
love for nature
love for classmates
love for school
love for food
love for respect
love for attention
reading books
bringing flowers

Me and My Country

Think of three things you love about your country, and talk about them. See whether the following items apply:

celebrating national holidays
watching fireworks

buying American products
celebrating New Year's Day
celebrating Martin Luther King Jr. Day
celebrating George Washington's birthday
celebrating Memorial Day
celebrating Independence Day
celebrating Labor Day
celebrating Columbus Day
celebrating Veterans Day
celebrating Thanksgiving Day
celebrating Christmas Day
watching American movies
enjoying American entertainment
knowing who our president is
keeping our American traditions

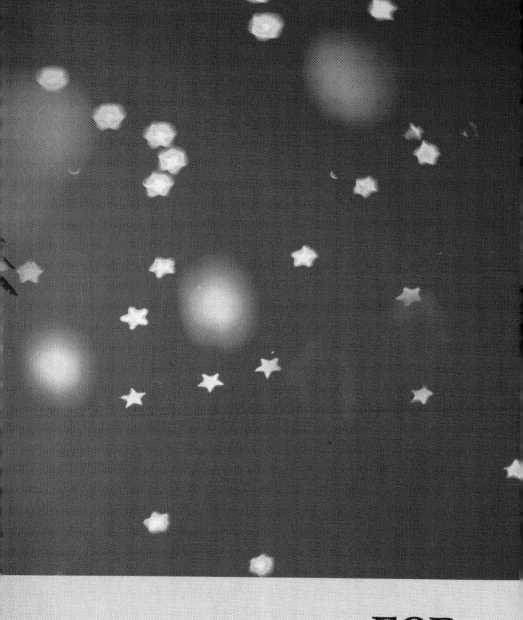

FOR
THIRD-GRADE
STUDENTS

My Birthday

Think of three things about your birthday, and write about them. See whether the following items apply:

a new thing you got for your birthday
this year you are choosing to do something new
the new good thing you want to do at this age is …
some fun summer activities for you this year will be …

I Am …

Think of three good things about yourself, and write about them. See whether the following items apply:

your time management skills
your reliability
your relationship management skills
the difference between wanting something or needing something
putting your seat belt on
doing good
being helpful
cleaning
taking care of your belongings and those things and people that are important to you, including the following:

- your birthday gifts
- your toys
- your friends
- your siblings
- your home
- your country

I Am Grateful for …

Think about three things you are grateful for, and write about them. See whether the following items apply:

> your family
> your country
> your looks
> your belongings
> your habits
> your friends
> your neighborhood
> your opportunities
> your school
> your classmates
> your cousins
> your siblings
> your health
> your happiness
> holidays
> summer vacation

Education is…

Think about three things that you agree with or know about education and write about them.

See whether the following items apply:

> It is easier to become a Doctor than to become a millionaire
> It is easier to make money, when you are a Doctor
> Education helps become more knowledgeable
> Education helps boost self-esteem
> Education is fun, if you are interested in it
> Education is a brain exercise
> Education helps solve problems easier
> Education can help earn respect

Education makes it easier to buy a lot of things you want
With education you can have your own business
Education is a prestige
Once you become a Doctor, you will be a Doctor for the rest
of your life
Education does not make you boring
Education can give you more than what money can
With education you can have money
With education you can have a stable job by the time you are
a middle aged person.
To become educated all you have to do is pick a subject and
do your homework
Many people can help you become educated
To become a Doctor all you need to do is continue your
education and do your homework
With education you may never become homeless
You can be educated as well as an entrepreneur
You can be educated as well as a millionaire
It is very easy to become educated if you have a favorite
subject
Your favorite subject in school is…
Your feelings about educated people are

I Feel Smart and/or Strong When I Am …

Think of three things that make you feel smart and/or strong, and
write about them. See whether the following items apply:

getting good grades
learning new words
choosing a better vocabulary
doing homework
finishing homework
exercising
when friends call
playing outdoors
when your parents say you've done a good job

when it's your birthday
thinking about things
putting your dishes in the sink

I Am Having Fun When I Am ...

Think of three fun things you like to do, and write about them. See whether the following items apply:

playing sports
camping
playing board games
watching games
dancing
making friends
talking to friends
having pets
swimming
meeting with relatives
traveling throughout the United States

Being a Hero Is When I Am ...

Think of three things that make you feel like a hero, and write about them. See whether the following items apply:

acting friendly
being able to express yourself without inappropriate words
being on time to school
being responsible for yourself
having fun
knowing what's good for you
not getting into trouble

My Culture ...

Think of three things that you love about your culture, and write about them. See whether the following items apply:

cultural values
cultural rituals
movies
music
food
presidents
entertainers
talk shows
radio shows
compare old movies and songs to new movies and songs
cartoons
fun community activities
magazines
camping
museums

The Support System in My Life ...

Think of three things you like about your family and friends, and write about them. See whether the following items apply:

socializing with your mom
socializing with your dad
socializing with your sister
socializing with your brother
socializing with your aunts
socializing with your uncles
socializing with your cousins
socializing with your friends
socializing with your family friends
socializing with your old neighbors
socializing with your new neighbors

socializing with your relatives
socializing with your friends at school
socializing with your teachers
socializing with your mom's friends' children
socializing with your dad's friends' children
socializing with a therapist you like
socializing with a good mentor

I Am a Good Child for My Family

Think of three good things you and your family members do for one another, and write about them. See whether the following items apply:

family as part of my community you live in
being grateful for having loving, caring parents
doing laundry
having a warm bed
having shoes that fit
washing your dishes
having food
having clothes
having a roof over your head
others listening to you sing
others listening to you
others playing sports with you
your parents putting your picture on the fridge
others giving you gifts
making your bed
saying thank you
helping to clean the table
helping with homework
putting your shoes where they are supposed to be
showing respect to the elderly

Self-Control Is When I Am ...

Think of three things you have self-control in, and write about them. See whether the following items apply:

> not taking cookies from cookie jars
> not talking during class activities
> exercising
> dressing up appropriately
> using clean words
> not arguing, but saying please
> keeping your cell phone on mute and controlling your phone (instead of your phone controlling you)
> not eating too many holiday candies
> putting away your shoes
> not interrupting
> not talking during class

I Am Responsible When I Am ...

Think of three of your responsibilities, and write about them. See whether the following items apply:

> doing your homework on time
> eating healthy food
> making your bed
> helping to clean the table after dinner
> helping your parents with chores
> putting your shoes in the closet
> tying your shoes
> not losing things

Girls Are Similar to and Different from Boys ...

Think of three things that are similar or different between boys and girls, and write about them. See whether the following items apply:

> choice of clothing
> shoes
> interests
> hobbies
> games
> dream job
> food
> exercise habits
> sport activities
> hair color
> eye color
> cars they drive
> last names
> signing abilities
> dancing abilities
> abilities to do school work
> abilities to put their shoes in their proper place
> abilities for washing the dishes

Growing Up

Think of three things about growing up, and write about them. See whether the following items apply:

> What is being a grown-up?
> Are you a grown-up yet?
> What are some of the things grown-ups do for themselves?
> What are some of the things grown-ups do for their family?
> What are some of the things grown-ups do for their relatives (hint: saying nice things)?
> What are some of the things grown-ups do for their friends?

What are some of the things grow-ups do for society?
What are some of the things grown-ups do for your country?

Good Person

Think of three things about any good person you know, and write about them. See whether the following items apply:

is whom you approve of as a good person
is whom Mom and Dad do not disapprove of
is kind
is helpful
is considerate
is responsible
does not harm others
does not let others hurt himself or herself
sets good examples
is nice to pets
waters the plants
is caring
is grateful
can say nice things

Love Is …

Think of three things you love, and write about them. See whether the following items apply:

love for family
love for friends
love for exercise
love for fun
love for country
love for entertainment
love for nature
love for classmates

love for school
love for food
love for respect
love for attention
reading books
bringing flowers

Me and My Country

Think of three things you love about your country, and write about them. See whether the following items apply:

celebrating and knowing about all national holidays
watching fireworks
buying American products
celebrating New Year's Day
celebrating Martin Luther King Jr. Day
celebrating George Washington's birthday
celebrating Memorial Day
celebrating Independence Day
celebrating Labor Day
celebrating Columbus Day
celebrating Veterans Day
celebrating Thanksgiving Day
celebrating Christmas
watching American movies
enjoying American entertainment
knowing who our president is
knowing which state you live in
knowing your state capital
keeping our American traditions

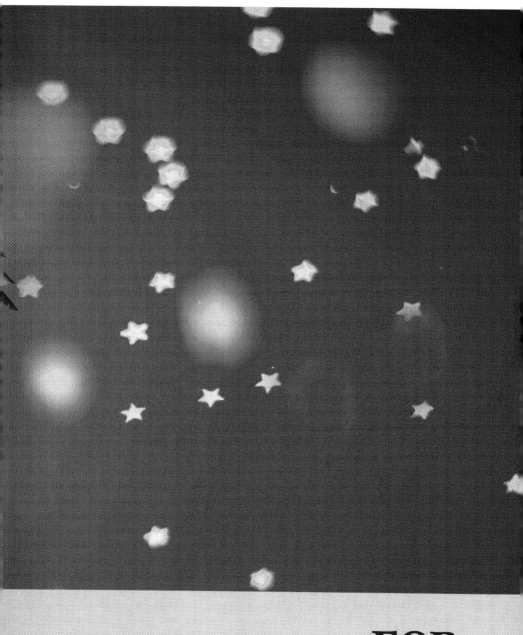

FOR
FOURTH-GRADE
STUDENTS

My Birthday

Think of three things about your birthday, and write about them. See whether the following items apply:

> new things for your new age
> a better life
> some of the fun summer activities for you this year will be ...
> new haircut
> new clothes
> new behavior

I Am ...

Think of three good things about yourself, and write about them. See whether the following items apply:

> all the good things about yourself that fit in this class
> your time management skills
> your reliability
> your relationship management skills
> the difference between wanting something or needing something
> putting your seat belt on
> doing good
> being helpful
> keeping your room clean

Taking care of your belongings and those things and people that are important to you, including the following:

- your birthday gifts
- your toys
- your friends
- your books
- your siblings

- your home
- your country

I Am Grateful for ...

Think about three things you are grateful for, and write about them.
See whether the following items apply:

> your family
> your country
> your looks
> your belongings
> your habits
> your friends
> your neighborhood
> your opportunities
> your school
> your classmates
> your cousins
> your siblings
> your health
> your happiness
> holidays
> summer vacation

Education is...

Think about three things that you agree with or know about education
and write about them. See whether the following items apply:

> It is easier to become a Doctor than to become a millionaire
> It is easier to make money, when you are a Doctor
> Education helps become more knowledgeable
> Education helps boost self-esteem
> Education is fun, if you are interested in it
> Education is a brain exercise

Education helps solve problems easier
Education can help earn respect
Education makes it easier to buy the things you want
With education you can have your own business
Education is a prestige
Once you become a Doctor, you will be a Doctor for the rest of your life
Education does not make you boring
Education can give you more than what money can
With education you can have money
With education you can have a stable job by the time you are a middle aged person.
To become educated all you have to do is pick a subject and do your homework
Many people can help you become educated
To become a Doctor all you need to do is continue your education and do your homework
With education you may never become homeless
You can be educated as well as an entrepreneur
You can be educated as well as a millionaire
It is very easy to become educated if you have a favorite subject
Your favorite subject in school is...
Your feelings about educated people are

I Feel Smart and/or Strong When ...

Think of three things that make you feel smart and/or strong, and write about them. See whether the following items apply:

getting good grades
learning new words
choosing a better vocabulary
doing homework
exercising
when friends call
when talking to friends

when playing outdoors
when your parents say you are doing a good job
when it's your birthday
thinking about things
putting the dishes in the sink after dinner

Being a Hero Is When I Am ...

Think of three things that make you feel like a hero, and write about them. See whether the following items apply:

acting friendly
riding a bike
ice-skating
acing your schoolwork
being able to express yourself with clean words
being on time to school
being responsible for yourself
having fun
knowing the cost and benefits of your actions
knowing what's good for you

My Culture ...

Think of three things you love about your culture, and write about them. See whether the following items apply:

cultural values
rituals
movies
music
food
presidents
entertainers
talk show hosts
radio hosts

compare old movies and songs to new movies and songs
cartoons
community fun
family activities
sporting events
Olympics
hot-air balloon festivals
tourists and tourist attractions
buildings and gardens
TV shows
museums
camping
magazines
books

The Support System in My Life ...

Think of three things you like about your family and friends, and write about them. See whether the following items apply:

socializing with your mom
socializing with your dad
socializing with your sister
socializing with your brother
socializing with your aunts
socializing with your uncles
socializing with your cousins
socializing with your friends
socializing with your old neighbors
socializing with your new neighbors
socializing with your relatives
socializing with your family friends
socializing with your friends at school
socializing with your teachers
socializing with your mom's friends' children
socializing with your dad's friends' children
socializing with a therapist you love

My Neighborhood

Think of three things about your neighborhood during different seasons and holidays of the year, and write about them. See whether the following items apply:

> the beautiful part of your neighborhood
> artwork
> buildings
> spending time with people
> trees
> flowers
> weather
> decorations on holidays

I Am a Good Child for My Family

Think of three good things that you and your family members do for one another, and write about them. See whether the following items apply:

> saying thank you
> having loving parents
> having caring parents
> doing laundry
> having a warm bed
> having shoes that fit
> washing your dishes
> having food
> having clothes
> having a roof over your head
> others listening to you sing
> others listening to you
> others playing sports with you
> others putting your picture up on the fridge
> buying gifts
> making your bed

helping clean the table
putting your shoes where they are supposed to be
showing respect to the elderly

Self-Control Is When I Am …

Think of three things you do that require self-control, and write about them. See whether the following items apply:

not taking cookies from cookie jars
not talking while class is in session
exercising
dressing up appropriately
not arguing, but using your words
keeping your cell phone on mute and controlling the phone
(instead of the phone controlling you)
not having too many holiday candies
putting away your shoes
not interrupting

I Am Responsible When I Am …

Think of three of your responsibilities, and write about them. See whether the following items apply:

doing your homework on time
eating healthy food
making your bed
helping to clean the table
putting your shoes in the closet
not losing things

I Am Having Fun When I Am ...

Think of three fun things, and write about them. See whether the following items apply:

playing sports
camping
playing board games
watching games
dancing
making friends
petting an animal
vacationing with your family
talking to your friends
swimming
meeting with relatives

Girls Are Similar to and Different from Boys ...

Think of three ways that boys and girls are similar or different, and write about them. See whether the following items apply:

abilities for washing the dishes
choice of clothing
shoes
interests
hobbies
games
dream job
food
exercise habits
sport activities
hair color
eye color
cars they drive
last names
signing abilities

dancing abilities
abilities to do school work
abilities to put their shoes in their proper place
boys are supportive when …
girls are supportive when …
valuable girl behaviors
valuable boy behaviors
some of the things guys do that make others feel valuable
some of the things girls do that make others feel valuable
some of the things that make girls special
some of the things that make boys special
choice of clothing

Growing Up

Think of three things grown-ups do, and write about them. See whether the following items apply:

What is being a grown-up?
Are you a grown-up yet?
What are some things grown-ups do for themselves?
What are some things grown-ups do for their family?
What are some things grown-ups do for their relatives (hint: saying nice things)?
What are some things grown-ups do for their friends?
What are some things grown-ups do for their society?
What are some things grown-ups do for your country?

Good Person

Think of three things that any good person you know does, and write about them. See whether the following items apply:

is whom you approve of as a good person
is whom Mom and Dad do not disapprove of
is kind

is helpful
is considerate
is responsible
does not harm others
does not let others hurt himself or herself
sets good examples
is nice to pets
waters the plants
is caring
is grateful
can say nice things

Love Is …

Think of three things you love, and write about them. See whether the following items apply:

love for family
love for friends
love for exercise
love for fun
love for country
love for entertainment
love for nature
love for classmates
love for school
love for food
love for respect
love for attention
reading books
reading children's poetry
bringing flowers

Think of three things you love about your country, and write about them. See whether the following items apply:

celebrating and knowing about all national holidays
watching fireworks
buying American products
celebrating New Year's Day
celebrating Martin Luther King Jr. Day
celebrating George Washington's birthday
celebrating Memorial Day
celebrating Independence Day
celebrating Labor Day
celebrating Columbus Day
celebrating Veterans Day
celebrating Thanksgiving Day
celebrating Christmas Day
watching American movies
enjoying American entertainments
knowing who our president is
knowing the names of all the states, including the one you live in
knowing all the names of the state capitals and yours too
keeping our American traditions

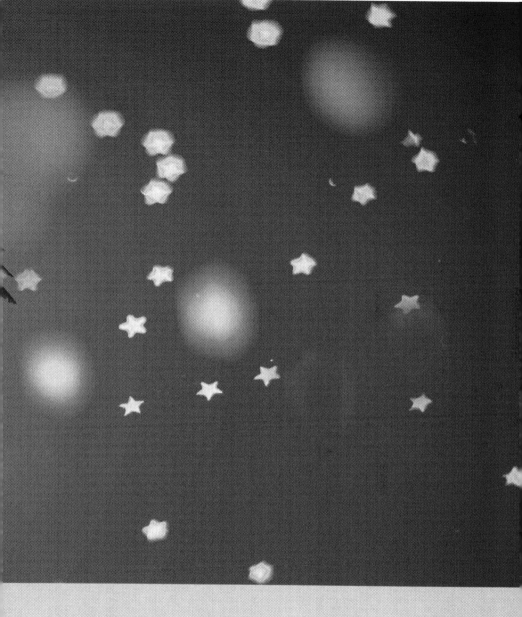

FOR FIFTH-GRADE STUDENTS

My Birthday

Think of three things about your birthday, and write about them. See whether the following items apply:

      a new present for your birthday
      choosing to have a better life
      choosing some new good thing for this year
      some of fun summer activities for you this year will be …

I Am …

Think of three good things about you, and write about them. See whether the following items apply:

      your time management skills
      your reliability
      your friends
      the difference between wanting something or needing something
      putting your seat belt on
      doing good
      being helpful for your family
      being helpful for your friends
      keeping your room clean
      taking care of your belongings
      your birthday gifts
      your books
      your siblings
      your home
      your country

I Am Grateful for ...

Think about three things you are grateful for, and write about them.
See whether the following items apply:

> your family
> your country
> your looks
> your belongings
> your habits
> your friends
> your neighborhood
> your opportunities
> your school
> your classmates
> your cousins
> your siblings
> your health
> your happiness
> holidays
> summer vacation

Education is...

Think about three things that you agree with or know about education
and write about them. See whether the following items apply:

> It is easier to become a Doctor than to become a millionaire
> It is easier to make money, when you are a Doctor
> Education helps become more knowledgeable
> Education helps boost self-esteem
> Education is fun, if you are interested in it
> Education is a brain exercise
> Education helps solve problems easier
> Education can help earn respect
> Education makes it easier to buy the things you want
> Education can help you find a more stable job

Education can help you have a more stable lifestyle
Education can help you have your own business
Education is a prestige
Once you become a Doctor, you will be a Doctor for the rest of your life
Education does not make you boring
Education can give you more than what money can
With education you can have money
With education you can satisfy your scientific interests
Education can make you a well-rounded person
With education you can have a stable job by the time you are 25 years old
To become educated all you have to do is pick a subject and commit
Many people can help you become educated
Education has a clear path
With education you may never become homeless
You can be educated as well as an entrepreneur
You can be educated as well as a millionaire
Education can open many doors for you
It is very easy to become educated if you have a favorite subject
Your favorite subject in school is…
Your feelings about educated people are

I Feel Smart and/or Strong When …

Think of three things that make you feel smart and/or strong, and write about them. See whether the following items apply:

getting good grades
learning new words
choosing a better vocabulary
doing homework
finishing homework
exercising

when friends call
when talking to friends
when playing outdoors
when parents say you've done a good job
when it's your birthday
when you think about good things
when you put the dishes in the sink after dinner

Being a Hero Is When I Am ...

Think of three things that make you feel like a hero, and write about them. See whether the following items apply:

acting friendly
riding a bike
ice-skating
acing your schoolwork
being able to express yourself without inappropriate words
being on time to school
being responsible for yourself
having fun
protecting your family name by saying nice things about your family
keeping high standards, especially the ones you appreciate in others
accepting the consequences of your actions
knowing what's good for you

My Culture ...

Think of three things you love about your culture, and write about them. See whether the following items apply:

cultural values
rituals
movies

music
food
presidents
entertainers
talk shows
radio shows
compare old movies and songs to new movies and songs
cartoons
community fun and family activities
sporting events
Olympics
hot-air balloon festivals
tourists and tourist attractions
buildings and gardens
TV shows
museums
camping
magazines
newspapers
books

The Support System in My Life ...

Think of three socializing activities you like, and write about them. See whether the following items apply:

socializing with your mom
socializing with your dad
socializing with your sister
socializing with your brother
socializing with your aunts
socializing with your uncles
socializing with your cousins
socializing with your friends
socializing with your neighbors
socializing with your relatives
socializing with your teachers

socializing with friends at school
socializing with your mom's friends' children
socializing with your dad's friends' children
socializing with a therapist you love
socializing with your good mentor

I Am a Good Child for My Family

Think of three good things you and your family members do for one another, and write about them. See whether the following items apply:

your family as part of your community you live in
having loving parents
having caring parents
doing laundry
having a warm bed
having shoes that fit
washing your dishes
having food
having clothes
having a roof over your head
others listening to you sing
others listening to you read
others playing sports with you
others putting your picture on the fridge
buying gifts
making your bed
saying thank you
helping to clean the table
putting your shoes where they are supposed to be
showing respect to the elderly

Self-Control Is When I Am ...

Think of three things you have self-control in, and write about them. See whether the following items apply:

> not getting into a fight but using your words
> not yelling but using your words
> staying quiet while class is in session
> exercising
> dressing up appropriately
> keeping your cell phone on mute and controlling the phone (instead of the phone controlling you)
> not eating too many holiday candies
> putting away your shoes
> not interrupting

I Am Responsible When I Am ...

Think of three of your responsibilities, and write about them. See whether the following items apply:

> doing your homework on time
> eating healthy food
> helping clean the table after dinner
> putting your shoes in the closet
> not losing things
> making your bed
> keeping your room clean
> helping around the house with chores

I Am Having Fun When I Am ...

Think of three fun things you like, and write about them. See whether the following items apply:

> playing sports

camping
playing board games
watching games
dancing
making friends
spending time with friends
petting an animal
vacationing with family
talking to friends
swimming
meeting with your relatives

I am Caring When I Am ...

Think of three nice things you do, and write about them. See whether the following items apply:

helping around the house
helping your siblings
feed the birds
ask about others' well-being
empathizing (not sympathizing) with people you like or love
complimenting someone
handling others' belongings appropriately
when you do something for your country

Girls Are Similar to and Different from Boys ...

Think of three ways that boys and girls are similar or different, and write about them. See whether the following items apply:

choice of clothing
shoes
interests
hobbies
games

dream job
food
exercise habits
sport activities
hair color
eye color
cars they drive
last names
signing abilities
dancing abilities
abilities to do school work
abilities to put their shoes in their proper place
abilities for washing the dishes
boys are supportive when …
girls are supportive when …
valuable girl behaviors
valuable boy behaviors
some of the things guys do that make others feel valuable
some of the things girls do that make others feel valuable
some of the things that make girls special
some of the things that make boys special

Growing Up

Think of three things about grown-ups, and write about them. See whether the following items apply:

What is being a grown-up?
Are you a grown-up yet?
What are some things you would like to do for yourself when you grow up?
What are some things you would like to do for your family when you grow up?
What are some things grown-ups do for their relatives (hint: saying nice things)?
What are some things you would like to do for your friends when you grow up?

What are some things you would like to do for your country when you grow up?

Good Person

Think of three things any good person you know does, and write about them. See whether the following items apply:

is whom you approve of as a good person
is whom Mom and Dad do not disapprove of
is kind
is helpful
is considerate
is responsible
does not harm others
does not let others hurt himself or herself
sets good examples
is nice to pets
waters the plants
is caring
is grateful
can say nice things

Love Is …

Think of three things you love, and write about them. See whether the following items apply:

love for family
love for friends
love for exercise
love for fun
love for country
love for entertainment
love for nature
love for classmates

love for school
love for food
love for respect
love for attention
reading books
bringing flowers

Me and My Country

Think of three things you love about your country, and write about them. See whether the following items apply:

caring for our country, America
celebrating and knowing about all national holidays
watching fireworks
buying American products
celebrating New Year's Day
celebrating Martin Luther King Jr. Day
celebrating George Washington's birthday
celebrating Memorial Day
celebrating Independence Day
celebrating Labor Day
celebrating Columbus Day
celebrating Veterans Day
celebrating Thanksgiving Day
celebrating Christmas Day
watching American movies
enjoying American entertainment
knowing who our president is
knowing the names of all the states, including the one you live in
knowing all the names of the state capitals and yours too
keeping our American traditions

FOR SIXTH-GRADE STUDENTS

My Birthday

Think of three things about your birthday, and write about them. See whether the following items apply:

getting a new thing for your birthday

choosing new good things this year

some of the fun summer activities for you this year are going to be …

I Am …

Think of three good things about yourself, and write about them. See whether the following items apply:

your time management skills

your reliability

your relationship management skills

the difference between wanting something or needing something

putting your seat belt on

doing good

being helpful

keeping your room clean

taking care of your belongings

your friends

your books

your siblings

your home

your country

I Am Grateful for ...

Think about three things you are grateful for, and write about them.
See whether the following items apply:

> your family
> your country
> your looks
> your belongings
> your habits
> your friends
> your neighborhood
> your opportunities
> your school
> your classmates
> your cousins
> your siblings
> your health
> your happiness
> holidays
> summer vacation

Education is...

Think about three things that you agree with or know about education
and write about them. See whether the following items apply:

> It is easier to become a Doctor than to become a millionaire
> It is easier to make money, when you are a Doctor
> Education helps become more knowledgeable
> Education helps boost self-esteem
> Education is fun, if you are interested in it
> Education is a brain exercise
> Education helps solve problems easier
> Education can help earn respect
> Education makes it easier to buy the things you want
> Education can help you find a more stable job

Education can help you have a more stable lifestyle
Education can help you have your own business
Education is a prestige
Once you become a Doctor, you will be a Doctor for the rest of your life
Education does not make you boring
Education can give you more than what money can
With education you can have money
With education you can satisfy your scientific interests
Education can make you a well-rounded person
With education you can have a stable job by the time you are 25 years old
To become educated all you have to do is pick a subject and commit
Many people can help you become educated
Education has a clear path
With education you may never become homeless
You can be educated as well as an entrepreneur
You can be educated as well as a millionaire
Education can open many doors for you
It is very easy to become educated if you have a favorite subject
Your favorite subject in school is...
Your feelings about educated people are

I Feel Smart and/or Strong When ...

Think of three things that make you feel smart and/or strong, and write about them. See whether the following items apply:

getting good grades
learning new words
choosing better vocabulary
doing homework
exercising
winning in a game

finishing homework

when friends call

spending time with friends

talking to friends

playing outdoors

when your parents say you did a good job

when it's your birthday

thinking about things

putting your dishes in the sink

getting attention from the opposite gender

Being a Hero Is When I Am …

Think of three things that make you feel like a hero, and write about them. See whether the following items apply:

being friendly

having friends

being able to express yourself without inappropriate words

appreciating values

riding a bike

ice-skating

hiking

acing your schoolwork

being on time to school

being responsible for yourself

not forgetting to have fun

protecting your family name by saying nice things about them

keeping high standards, especially the ones you appreciate in others

knowing the cost and benefits for your actions

knowing the consequences of your actions

knowing what's good for you

showing gratitude to your family

buying made-in-the-USA products

keeping a good reputation within your family

keeping a good reputation in your school
keeping a good reputation with friends
keeping a good reputation with relatives

My Culture ...

Think of three things you love about our culture, and write about them. See whether the following items apply:

cultural values
cultural rituals
movies
music
food
presidents
entertainers
talk show hosts
radio hosts
compare old movies and songs to new movies and songs
cartoons
community fun and family activities
sporting events
Olympics
economy
hot-air balloon festivals
film events, red-carpet awards
tourists and tourist attractions
buildings and gardens
Renaissance fairs
fun college courses
TV shows
museums
camping
magazines
newspapers
books

Think of three socializing activities you like, and write about them. See whether the following items apply:

> socializing with your mother
> socializing with your father
> socializing with your sister
> socializing with your brother
> socializing with your aunts
> socializing with your uncles
> socializing with your cousins
> socializing with your friends
> socializing with your friends' families
> socializing with your new and old neighbors
> socializing with your relatives
> socializing with your family friends
> socializing with your friends at school
> socializing with your classmates
> socializing with your teachers
> socializing with your mother's friends
> socializing with your mother's friends' children
> socializing with your father's friends
> socializing with your father's friends' children
> socializing with a therapist you love
> socializing with a good mentor

I Am a Good Child for My Family

Think of three good things you and your family members do for one another, and write about them. See whether the following items apply:

> your family as part of your community
> being grateful
> having loving parents
> having caring parents

doing laundry
having a warm bed
having shoes that fit
washing your dishes
having food
having clothes
having a roof over your head
others listening to you sing
others listening to you reading poetry
others playing sports with you
others putting your picture on the fridge
buying gifts
making your bed
cleaning the table
putting your shoes and clothes where they are supposed
to be
showing respect to the elderly

Self-Control Is When I Am …

Think of three things you have self-control in, and write about them.
See whether the following items apply:

not harming yourself
not harming others
choosing your words wisely
not getting into a fight
using your words and not screaming
listening quietly during class activities
exercising
dressing up appropriately
keeping your cell phone on mute and controlling the phone
(instead of the phone controlling you)
not eating too many holiday candies
putting away your shoes and clothes
not interrupting

I Am Responsible When I Am ...

Think of three responsibilities you have, and write about them. See whether the following items apply:

> doing your homework on time
> eating healthy food
> cleaning the table after dinner
> putting your shoes and clothes where they belong
> not losing things
> making your bed
> driving responsibly
> helping around the house with the chores

I Am Caring When I Am ...

Think of three good things you do that make you feel like a caring person, and write about them. See whether the following items apply:

> helping around the house
> helping your siblings
> feed the birds
> ask about others' well-being
> empathizing (not sympathizing) with people you like or love
> complimenting someone
> handling others' belongings appropriately
> when you do something for your country

When I Am Having Fun and It Is Healthy ...

Think of three healthy activities you love doing, and write about them. See whether the following items apply:

> playing sports
> camping

playing board games
watching games
singing
dancing
making friends
spending time with friends
petting an animal
vacationing with family
swimming
meeting with relatives
traveling throughout the United States

Girls Are Similar to and Different from Boys …

Think of three ways boys and girls are similar or different, and write about them. See whether the following items apply:

choice of clothing
shoes
interests
hobbies
games
dream job
food
exercise habits
sport activities
hair color
eye color
cars they drive
last names
signing abilities
dancing abilities
abilities to do school work
abilities to put their shoes in their proper place
abilities for washing the dishes
boys are supportive when …
girls are supportive when …

valuable girl behaviors
valuable boy behaviors
some of the things guys do that make others feel valuable
some of the things girls do that make others feel valuable
some of the things that make girls special
some of the things that make boys special

Growing Up

Think of three things that constitute being a grown-up, and write about them. See whether the following items apply:

What is being a grown-up?
Are you a grown-up?
What are some things grown-ups do for themselves?
What are some things grown-ups do for their families?
What are some things grown-ups do for their relatives (hint: saying nice things about them)?
What are some things grown-ups do for their friends?
What are some things you do for your friends?
What are some things grown-ups do for your country?
What are some things you would love to do for your country?

Good Person

Think of three things that constitute a good person for you, and write about them. See whether the following items apply:

is whom you approve of as a good person
is whom Mom and Dad do not disapprove of
is kind
is helpful
is considerate
is responsible
does not harm others
does not let others hurt himself or herself

sets good examples
is nice to pets
waters the plants
is caring
is grateful
can say nice things
understanding
nice
work out
work for their families
do good deeds

Love Is …

Think of three things you love, and write about them. See whether the following items apply:

love for family
love for friends
love for exercising
love for fun
love for country
love for entertainment
love for nature
love for classmates
love for school
love for food
love for respect
love for attention
love for reading poetry
bringing flowers
walking side by side with someone special
sightseeing
listening
expressing values
having lunch with family

Think of three things you love about your country, and write about them. See whether the following items apply:

caring for our country, America
watching fireworks
buying American products
celebrating New Year's Day
celebrating Martin Luther King Jr. Day
celebrating George Washington's birthday
celebrating Memorial Day
celebrating Independence Day
celebrating Labor Day
celebrating Columbus Day
celebrating Veterans Day
celebrating Thanksgiving Day
celebrating Christmas Day
watching American movies
enjoying American entertainment
knowing who our president is
knowing the names of all the states, including the one you live in
knowing all the names of the state capitals and yours too
keeping our American traditions

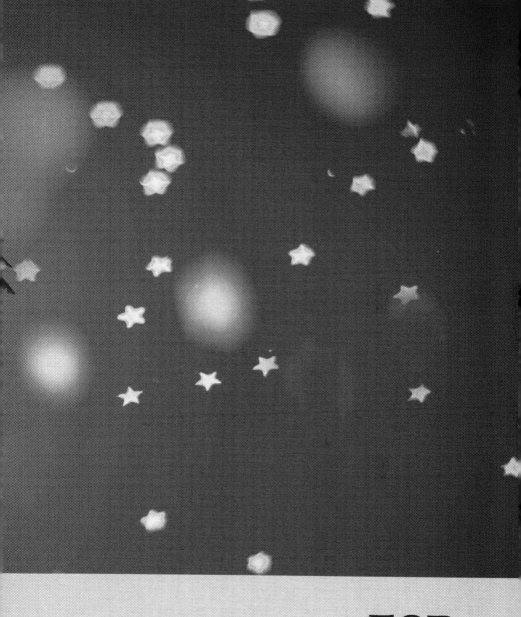

FOR
SEVENTH-GRADE
STUDENTS

My Birthday

Think of three things about your birthday, and write about them. See whether the following items apply:

> a new thing for your birthday
> choosing something good and new for this year
> choosing an improved lifestyle
> a new good thing you want to do at this age is ...
> some fun summer activities for this year for you will be ...

I Am ...

Think of three good things about yourself, and write about them. See whether the following items apply:

> your time management skills
> your reliability
> your relationship management skills
> being true to yourself
> knowing the difference between wanting something and needing something
> putting your seat belt on
> doing a good deed
> being helpful for your family
> being helpful for your friends
> keeping your room clean
> taking care of your belongings
> your friends
> your books
> your siblings
> your home
> your country

I Am Grateful for ...

Think about three things you are grateful for, and write about them. See whether the following items apply:

> your family
> your country
> your looks
> your belongings
> your habits
> your friends
> your neighborhood
> your opportunities
> your school
> your classmates
> your cousins
> your siblings
> your health
> your happiness
> holidays
> summer vacation
> your doctors

Education is...

Think about three things that you agree with or know about education and write about them. See whether the following items apply:

> It is easier to become a Doctor than to become a millionaire
> It is easier to make money, when you are a Doctor
> Education helps become more knowledgeable
> Education helps boost self-esteem
> Education is fun, if you are interested in it
> Education is a brain exercise
> Education helps solve problems easier
> Education can help earn respect
> Education makes it easier to buy the things you want

Education can help you find a more stable job
Education can help you have a more stable lifestyle
Education can help you have your own business
Education is a prestige
Once you become a Doctor, you will be a Doctor for the rest of your life
Education does not make you boring
Education can give you more than what money can
With education you can have money
With education you can satisfy your scientific interests
Education can make you a well-rounded person
With education you can have a stable job by the time you are 25 years old
To become educated all you have to do is pick a subject and commit
Many people can help you become educated
Education has a clear path
With education you may never become homeless
You can be educated as well as an entrepreneur
You can be educated as well as a millionaire
Education can open many doors for you
It is very easy to become educated if you have a favorite subject
Your favorite subject in school is…
Your feelings about educated people are

I Feel Smart and/or Strong When I Am …

Think of three things that make you feel smart and/or strong, and write about them. See whether the following items apply:

    getting good grades
    learning new words
    choosing a better vocabulary
    doing your homework
    finishing your homework

exercising

when friends call

when you feel older

spending time with friends

playing outdoors

when your parents say you have done a good job

when it's your birthday

thinking about things you have done

putting the dishes in the sink

when you get attention from the opposite gender

Being a Hero Is When I Am ...

Think of three things you do that make you feel like a hero, and write about them. See whether the following items apply:

being friendly

being able to express yourself without inappropriate words

appreciating values

riding a bike

riding in a car

ice-skating

skydiving

acing your schoolwork

being on time to school

being responsible for yourself

not forgetting to have fun

protecting your family name by saying nice things about them

emotional and/or physical support

keeping high standards, especially the ones you appreciate in others

know the cost and benefits for your actions

knowing what's good for you

showing gratitude to your family

buying products made in the United States

maintaining a good reputation within your family

maintaining a good reputation in school
maintaining a good reputation with your friends
maintaining a good reputation with your relatives

My Culture …

Think of three things you love about our culture, and write about
them. See whether the following items apply:

cultural values
cultural rituals
movies
music
food
presidents
entertainers
talk shows
talk show hosts
radio shows
radio show hosts
compare old movies to new movies
country songs
modern songs
cartoons
community fun and family activities
sporting events
Olympics
economy
hot-air balloon festivals
film events, red-carpet awards
festivals
tourists and tourist attractions
structures and establishments
botanical gardens and arboretums
buildings and gardens
Renaissance fairs
fun colleges

fun college courses
TV shows
museums
camping
magazines
newspapers
books
highly valued education

The Support System in My Life ...

Think of three socializing activities you like, and write about them. See whether the following items apply:

socializing with your mother
socializing with your father
socializing with your sister
socializing with your brother
socializing with your aunts
socializing with your uncles
socializing with your cousins
socializing with your friends
socializing with your friends' families
socializing with new and old neighbors
socializing with your relatives
socializing with your family friends
socializing with your friends at school
socializing with your teachers
socializing with your mother's friends
socializing with your mother's friends' children
socializing with your father's friends
socializing with your father's friends' children
socializing with a good therapist you love
socializing with a good mentor

Friendship Is ...

Think of three things that pertain to friendship, and write about
them. See whether the following items apply:

noticing values
noticing your family values
understanding your values
friends appreciating your values
friends appreciating your family's values

Growing Up

Think of three things that constitute being a grown-up, and write
about them. See whether the following items apply:

What is being a grown-up?
Are you a grown-up yet?
What are some things you would like to do for yourself when
you are a grown-up?
What are some things you would like to do for your family
when you are a grown-up?
What are some things you would like to do for your relatives
when you are a grown-up?
What are some things you would like to do for your friends
when you are a grown-up?
What are some things you would like to do for your country
when you are a grown-up?
What are some high values and standards grown-ups have?

Relationship Is ...

Think of three things you love about relationships, and write about
them. See whether the following items apply:

understanding each other

caring for each other
noticing each other
talking to each other
talking each other up
supporting each other
being drawn to each other
wanting to have the same lifestyle as each other
liking each other
dancing with each other

Movies

Think of three things you love and find appropriate to share in this class, about watching a rated G movie, and write about them. See whether the following items apply:

favorite movies
favorite scenes
favorite line in a movie
favorite music in a movie
favorite actor or actress in a movie
favorite outfit in a movie
favorite behavior in a movie

I Am a Good Person for My Family

Think of three good things you and your family do for each other, and write about them. See whether the following items apply:

family as a good part of my community I live in
some of the things parents do for family
some of the things you will do for your children when you are a parent
being grateful
having loving parents
having caring parents

doing laundry
having a warm bed
having shoes that fit
washing your dishes
having food
having clothes
having a roof over your head
others playing sports with you
others putting your picture on the fridge
buying gifts
making your bed
cleaning the table
putting shoes and clothes where they are supposed to be
showing respect to the elderly

Self-Control Is When I Am …

Think of three things you have self-control in, and write about them.
See whether the following items apply:

not harming yourself
not harming others
using appropriate words and not getting into a fight
using your words and not screaming
listening quietly during the class
exercising
dressing up appropriately
keeping your cell phone on mute and controlling your phone
(instead of your phone controlling you)
not having too many holiday candies
putting away your shoes
not interrupting

I Am Responsible When I Am ...

Think of three things you are responsible for, and write about them. See whether the following items apply:

doing your homework in a timely manner
eating healthy food
cleaning the table
putting your shoes in the closet
not losing things
maintaining a clean room
maintaining a clean car

I Am Caring When I Am ...

Think of three things you do that make you feel like a caring person, and write about them. See whether the following items apply:

helping friends
helping around the house
helping your siblings
feed the birds
ask about others' well-being
empathizing (not sympathizing) with people you like or love
complimenting someone
handling others' belongings appropriately
when you do something for your country

When I Am Having Fun and It Is Healthy ...

Think of three healthy, fun activities you love that are also appropriate for this class, and write about them. See whether the following items apply:

playing sports
camping

playing board games
watching games
dancing
making friends
petting an animal
vacationing with your family
talking to friends
swimming
meeting with your relatives
traveling throughout the United States

Girls Are Similar to and Different from Boys ...

Think of three ways that boys and girls are similar or different, and write about them. See whether the following items apply:

choice of clothing
shoes
interests
hobbies
games
dream job
food
exercise habits
sport activities
hair color
eye color
cars they drive
last names
signing abilities
dancing abilities
abilities to do school work
abilities to put their shoes in their proper place
abilities for washing the dishes
boys are supportive when ...
girls are supportive when ...
valuable girl behaviors

valuable boy behaviors
some of the things guys do that make others feel valuable
some of the things girls do that make others feel valuable
some of the things that make girls special
some of the things that make boys special
attention, goals, self-presentation, self-care, etc.

Good Person

Think of three things that constitute a good person, and write about them. See whether the following items apply. See whether the following items apply:

is whom you approve of as a good person
is whom Mom and Dad do not disapprove of
is kind
is helpful
is considerate
is responsible
does not harm others
does not let others hurt himself or herself
sets good examples
is nice to pets
waters the plants
is caring
is grateful
can say nice things

Love Is …

Think of three things you love, and write about them. See whether the following items apply:

love for family
love for country
love for friends

love for exercise
love for fun
love for entertainment
love for nature
love for classmates
love for school
love for food
love for respect
love for attention
love for reading poetry
love for bringing flowers
walking side by side with a special someone
sightseeing
listening to friends talk
expressing values
having lunch with family
entertainment

Me and My Country

Think of three things you love about your country, and write about them. See whether the following items apply:

caring for our country, America
watching fireworks
buying American products
celebrating New Year's Day
celebrating Martin Luther King Jr. Day
celebrating George Washington's birthday
celebrating Memorial Day
celebrating Independence Day
celebrating Labor Day
celebrating Columbus Day
celebrating Veterans Day
celebrating Thanksgiving Day
celebrating Christmas Day
watching American movies

enjoying American entertainment
knowing who our president is
knowing the names of all the states, including the one you
live in
knowing all the names of the state capitals and yours too
keeping our American traditions
loving everything America has to offer today
loving all the opportunities you have in America

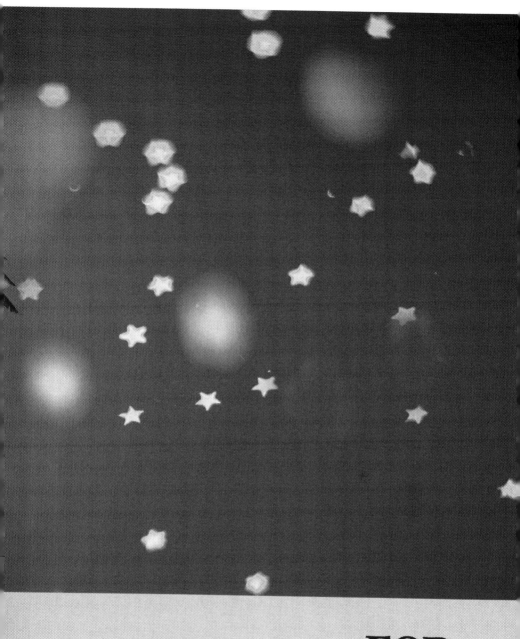

FOR
EIGHTH-GRADE
STUDENTS

My Birthday

Think of three things about your birthday, and write about them. See whether the following items apply:

a new thing for your birthday
choosing to have an improved lifestyle for this year
choosing something new this year
some of the fun summer activities for you this year will be ...

I Am ...

Think of three good things about yourself that are appropriate for this class, and write about them. See whether the following items apply:

your time management skills
your reliability
your relationship management skills
being true to yourself
knowing the difference between wanting something and needing something
putting your seat belt on
doing good
being helpful
keeping your room clean
taking care of your belongings
your birthday gifts
your friends
your books
your siblings
your home
our country

I Am Grateful for ...

Think about three things you are grateful for, and write about them. See whether the following items apply:

> your family
> your country
> your looks
> your belongings
> your habits
> your friends
> your neighborhood
> your opportunities
> your school
> your classmates
> your cousins
> your siblings
> your health
> your happiness
> holidays
> summer vacation
> your doctors
> your friends' personalities
> your lifestyle

Education is...

Think about three things that you agree with or know about education and write about them. See whether the following items apply:

> It is easier to become a Doctor than to become a millionaire
> It is easier to make money, when you are a Doctor
> Education helps become more knowledgeable
> Education helps boost self-esteem
> Education is fun, if you are interested in it
> Education is a brain exercise
> Education helps solve problems easier

Education can help earn respect

Education makes it easier to buy the things you want

Education can help you find a more stable job

Education can help you have a more stable lifestyle

Education can help you have your own business

Education is a prestige

Once you become a Doctor, you will be a Doctor for the rest of your life

Education does not make you boring

Education can give you more than what money can

With education you can have money

With education you can satisfy your scientific interests

Education can make you a well-rounded person

With education you can have a stable job by the time you are 25 years old

To become educated all you have to do is pick a subject and commit

Many people can help you become educated

Education has a clear path

With education you may never become homeless

You can be educated as well as an entrepreneur

You can be educated as well as a millionaire

Education can open many doors for you

It is very easy to become educated if you have a favorite subject

Your favorite subject in school is…

Your feelings about educated people are

I Feel Smart and/or Strong When …

Think of three things that make you feel smart and/or strong, and write about them. See whether the following items apply:

getting good grades
learning new words
choosing better vocabulary

doing homework
finishing homework
exercising
when friends call
when you feel older
spending time with friends
talking to friends
playing outdoors
when your parents say you are doing a good job
when it's your birthday
thinking about things you have done
putting the dishes in the sink
getting attention from the opposite gender

My Culture ...

Think of three things you love about your culture, and write about them. See whether the following items apply:

cultural values
cultural rituals
movies
music
food
presidents
entertainers
talk shows
talk show hosts
radio shows
compare old movies to new movies
country songs
modern songs
cartoons
community fun and family activities
sporting events
Olympics
stadiums

economy
hot-air balloon festivals
film events, red-carpet awards
festivals
tourists and tourist attractions
structures and establishments
botanical gardens and arboretums
buildings and gardens
Renaissance fairs
fun college programs and courses
museums
comedy and humor
TV shows
camping
magazines
newspapers
books and novels
highly valued education

Being a Hero Is When I Am ...

Think of three things you do that make you feel like a hero, and write about them. See whether the following items apply:

buying made-in-the-USA products
being friendly
being able to express yourself without inappropriate words
appreciating values
riding a bike
ice-skating
acing your schoolwork
being able to express yourself without inappropriate words
being on time to school and appointments
being responsible for yourself
not forgetting fun
protecting your family name by saying nice things about your family members

emotional and/or physical support

keeping high standards, especially the ones you appreciate in others

knowing the cost and benefits of your actions

knowing what's good for you

showing gratitude to your family

maintaining a good reputation within your family

maintaining a good reputation in school

maintaining a good reputation with friends

maintaining a good reputation with relatives

the knowledge of maintaining a good reputation in your workplace

The Support System in My Life ...

Think of three socializing activities you like, and write about them. See whether the following items apply:

socializing with your mother
socializing with your father
socializing with your sister
socializing with your brother
socializing with your aunts
socializing with your uncles
socializing with your cousins
socializing with your friends
socializing with your friends' families
socializing with new and old neighbors
socializing with your relatives
socializing with your family friends
socializing with your friends at school
socializing with your teachers
socializing with your mother's friends
socializing with your mother's friends' children
socializing with your father's friends
socializing with your father's friends' children
socializing with a good therapist you love

socializing with a good mentor

I Am a Good Person for My Family

Think of three good things you and your family members do for one another, and write about them. See whether the following items apply:

awareness of family as part of your community
some of the things your parents do for your family
some of the things you will do for your children when you are a parent
being grateful
having loving parents
having caring parents
doing laundry
having a warm bed
having shoes that fit
washing your dishes
having food
having clothes
having a roof over your head
others listening to your singing
others listening to you reading poetry
others playing sports with you
others putting your picture on the fridge
buying gifts
making your bed
cleaning the table
doing your homework
putting your shoes where they are supposed to be
showing respect to the elderly

Self-Control Is When I Am ...

Think of three things you have self-control in, and write about them. See whether the following items apply:

> not harming yourself
> not harming others
> using your words and not getting into a fight
> using your words and not screaming
> not talking and instead listening during class
> exercising
> dressing appropriately
> keeping your cell phone on mute and controlling your phone (instead of your phone controlling you)
> not eating too many holiday candies
> putting away your clothes and shoes
> not interrupting

I Am Responsible When I Am ...

Think about three things that you take responsibility for, and write about them. See whether the following items apply:

> doing your homework in a timely manner
> eating healthy food
> cleaning the table
> putting shoes and clothes in the closet
> not losing things

I Am Caring When I Am ...

Think of three things that you care about and that make you feel like a caring person, and write about them. See whether the following items apply:

> helping friends

helping around the house
helping your siblings
feed the birds
ask about others' well-being
empathizing (not sympathizing) with people you like or love
complimenting someone
handling others' belongings appropriately
when you do something for your country

When I Am Having Fun and It Is Healthy ...

Think of three healthy, fun activities you love that are also appropriate for this class, and write about them. See whether the following items apply:

playing sports
camping
playing board games
watching games
dancing
making friends
petting an animal
vacationing with family
talking to friends
swimming
meeting with relatives
traveling throughout the United States

Girls Are Similar to and Different from Boys ...

Think of three ways that boys and girls are similar or different, and write about them. See whether the following items apply:

choice of clothing
shoes
interests

hobbies
games
dream job
food
exercise habits
sport activities
hair color
eye color
cars they drive
last names
signing abilities
dancing abilities
abilities to do school work
abilities to put their shoes in their proper place
abilities for washing the dishes
boys are supportive when …
girls are supportive when …
valuable girl behaviors
valuable boy behaviors
some of the things guys do that make others feel valuable
some of the things girls do that make others feel valuable
some of the things that make girls special
some of the things that make boys special
attention, goals, self-presentation, self-care, attire, etc.

Growing Up

Think of three things that constitute being grown-up, and write about them. See whether the following items apply:

What is being a grown-up?
Are you a grown-up yet?
What are some things you would like to do for yourself when you are a grown-up?
What are some things you would like to do for your family when you are a grown-up?

What are some things you would like to do for your relatives when you are a grown-up?
What are some things you would like to do for your friends when you are a grown-up?
What are some things you would like to do for your country when you are a grown-up?
What are some of the high standards grown-ups have?

Relationship Is ...

Think of three things you love about relationships, and write about them. See whether the following items apply:

understanding each other
caring for each other
noticing each other
talking to each other
talking each other up
supporting each other
being drawn to each other
wanting to have the same lifestyle as each other
liking each other
dancing with each other

Movies

Think of three things you love and find appropriate to share in this class, about watching a rated G movie, and write about them. See whether the following items apply:

favorite movies
favorite scenes
favorite line in a movie
favorite music in a movie
favorite actor or actress in a movie
favorite outfit in a movie

favorite behavior in a movie

Honorable Person

Think of three things that constitute an honorable person, and write about them. You can also write about anyone you know. See whether the following items apply:

> keeping a promise
> being honest
> valuing self
> dedicating yourself to a valuable cause
> not doing something in secret that you would not admit in public
> not harming
> maintaining boundaries
> not letting others step all over you
> respecting others as you respect yourself
> earning respect
> forgiving
> taking the high road by letting little things go

Love Is …

Think of three things you love, and write about them. See whether the following items apply:

> love for family
> love for friends
> love for exercise
> love for fun
> love for country
> love for entertainment
> love for nature
> love for classmates
> love for school

love for food
love for respect
love for attention
reading poetry
bringing flowers
walking with a special someone
sightseeing
listening to a friend
expressing values
having lunch with family
entertainment

Me and My Country

Think of three things you love about your country, and write about them. See whether the following items apply:

everything America has to offer
all the opportunities you have in America
caring for our country, America
watching fireworks
buying American products
celebrating New Year's Day
celebrating Martin Luther King Jr. Day
celebrating George Washington's birthday
celebrating Memorial Day
celebrating Independence Day
celebrating Labor Day
celebrating Columbus Day
celebrating Veterans Day
celebrating Thanksgiving Day
celebrating Christmas Day
watching American movies
enjoying American entertainment
knowing who our president is
knowing the names of all the states, including the one you live in

knowing all the names of the state capitals and yours too
keeping our American traditions
protecting your country when you are a grown-up
loving the people in your country
your country, the best place in the world
protecting your country and the people here every day

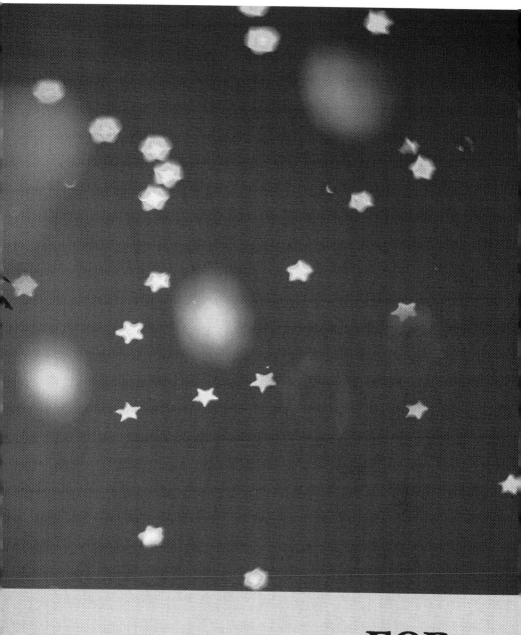

FOR
NINTH-GRADE
STUDENTS

My Birthday

Think of three things about your birthday, and write about them. See whether the following items apply:

> a new thing for your birthday
> choosing something new and good this year
> choosing something good to improve life with this year
> some of the fun summer activities for you this year will be ...

I Am ...

Think of three of your values that you find are appropriate for this class, and write about them. See whether the following items apply:

> your time management skills
> your reliability
> your relationship management skills
> being true to yourself
> knowing the difference between wanting something or needing something
> putting your seat belt on
> doing good
> being helpful
> keeping your room clean
> taking care of your belongings
> your birthday gifts
> your friends
> your books
> your siblings
> your home
> our country

I Am Grateful for …

Think about three things you are grateful for, and write about them.
See whether the following items apply:

> your family
> your country
> your looks
> your belongings
> your habits
> your friends
> your neighborhood
> your opportunities
> your school
> your classmates
> your cousins
> your siblings
> your health
> your happiness
> holidays
> summer vacation
> your doctors
> your friends' personalities
> your lifestyle

Education is…

Think about three things that you agree with or know about education
and write about them. See whether the following items apply:

> It is easier to become a Doctor than to become a millionaire
> It is easier to make money, when you are a Doctor
> Education helps become more knowledgeable
> Education helps boost self-esteem
> Education is fun, if you are interested in it
> Education is a brain exercise
> Education helps solve problems easier

Education can help earn respect
Education makes it easier to buy the things you want
Education can help you find a more stable job
Education can help you have a more stable lifestyle
Education can help you have your own business
Education is a prestige
Once you become a Doctor, you will be a Doctor for the rest of your life
Education does not make you boring
Education can give you more than what money can
With education you can have money
With education you can satisfy your scientific interests
Education can make you a well-rounded person
With education you can have a stable job by the time you are 25 years old
To become educated all you have to do is pick a subject and commit
Many people can help you become educated
Education has a clear path
With education you may never become homeless
You can be educated as well as an entrepreneur
You can be educated as well as a millionaire
Education can open many doors for you
It is very easy to become educated if you have a favorite subject
Your favorite subject in school is…
Your feelings about educated people are

I Feel Smart and/or Strong When …

Think of three things that make you feel smart and/or strong, and write about them. See whether the following items apply:

getting good grades
learning new words
choosing a better vocabulary

doing homework
finishing homework
exercising
when friends call
when you feel older
spending time with friends
talking to friends
playing outdoors
when your parents say you did a good job
when it's your birthday
thinking about things you have done
putting your dishes in the sink
getting attention from the opposite gender

My Culture

Think of three valuable things about our culture that you love, and write about them. See whether the following items apply:

cultural values
cultural rituals
movies
music
food
presidents
key figures
entertainers
talk shows
radio shows
compare old movies to new movies
country songs
modern songs
cartoons
community fun and family activities
sporting events
Olympics
stadiums

valued sports events
economy
hot-air balloon festivals
film events, red-carpet awards
festivals
tourists and tourist attractions
structures and establishments
botanical gardens and arboretums
buildings and gardens
Renaissance fairs
fun college programs and courses
museums
comedy and humor
TV shows
camping
magazines
newspapers
books and best novels of the twentieth century
highly valued education

Work

Think of three values that come in handy in a work environment, and write about them. See whether the following items apply:

favorite work
favorite pay
friendly colleagues compared to friendly classmates and other friends
rules at work
obedience for work
knowledge of compliance with work ethics
friendly boss
friendly you
purpose of your work
contribution to society with your work

Being a Hero Is When I Am ...

Think of three values and standards that make you feel like a hero, and write about them. See whether the following items apply:

knowing honor
knowing respect
knowing discipline
being friendly
driving responsibly
not paying too much for car insurance
ability to get along with people without causing problems
being able to express yourself without use of inappropriate words
appreciating values
driving a car
ice-skating
hiking
acing your schoolwork
being on time to school
being responsible for yourself
not forgetting fun
protecting your family name by saying nice things about them
emotional and/or physical support
keeping high standards, especially the ones you appreciate in others
promoting good behavior
knowing your priorities
knowing the cost and benefits of your actions
knowing what's good for you

Think of three socializing activities you like, and write about them. See whether the following items apply:

> socializing with your mother
> socializing with your father
> socializing with your sister
> socializing with your brother
> socializing with your aunts
> socializing with your uncles
> socializing with your cousins
> socializing with your friends
> socializing with your friends' families
> socializing with new and old neighbors
> socializing with your relatives
> socializing with your family friends
> socializing with your friends at school
> socializing with your teachers
> socializing with your mother's friends
> socializing with your mother's friends' children
> socializing with your father's friends
> socializing with your father's friends' children
> socializing with a good therapist you love
> socializing with a good mentor

I Am a Good Person for My Family

Think of three good things that you and your family do for one another, and write about them. See whether the

> family as part of the community you live in
> some of the things your parents do for your family
> some of the things you will do for your children when you are a parent
> being grateful
> having loving parents

having caring parents
doing laundry
having a warm bed
having shoes that fit
washing your dishes
cooking your food
having clothes
having a roof over your head
others playing sports with you
buying gifts
making your bed
cleaning your table
putting your clothes and shoes where they are supposed to be
showing respect to the elderly

Self-Control Is When I Am ...

Think of three things you have self-control in, and write about them. See whether the following items apply:

not harming yourself
not harming others
using your words and not getting into a fight
using your words and not screaming
listening to the teacher, instead of making noise during the class
exercising
dressing appropriately
keeping your cell phone on mute and controlling your phone (instead of your phone controlling you)
not having too many holiday candies
putting away your shoes
not interrupting
understanding that no means no

I Am Responsible When I Am ...

Think of three valuable things you take responsibility for, and write about them. See whether the following items apply:

doing your homework in a timely manner
eating healthy food
cleaning the table
putting your shoes in the closet
not losing things
driving responsibly and safely
maintaining a clean home
maintaining a clean car
helping around the house

I Am Caring When I Am ...

Think of three things that you care about and that make you feel like a caring person, and write about them. See whether the following items apply:

helping friends
helping around the house
helping my siblings
feed the birds
ask about others' well-being
empathizing (not sympathizing) with people you like or love
complimenting someone
handling others' belongings appropriately
when you do something for your country

When I Am Having Fun and It Is Healthy ...

Think of three healthy, fun activities you love that are also appropriate for this class, and write about them. See whether the following items apply:

> playing sports
> camping
> playing board games
> watching games
> dancing
> making friends
> petting an animal
> vacationing with family
> talking to friends
> swimming
> meeting with relatives
> traveling throughout the United States

Girls Are Similar to and Different from Boys ...

Think of three ways that boys and girls are similar or different, and write about them. See whether the following items apply:

> choice of clothing
> shoes
> interests
> hobbies
> games
> dream job
> food
> exercise habits
> sport activities
> hair color
> eye color
> cars they drive
> last names

signing abilities
dancing abilities
abilities to do school work
abilities to put their shoes in their proper place
abilities for washing the dishes
boys are supportive when …
girls are supportive when …
valuable girl behaviors
valuable boy behaviors
some of the things guys do that make others feel valuable
some of the things girls do that make others feel valuable
some of the things that make girls special
some of the things that make boys special
attention, goals, self-presentation, self-care, attire, etc.

Growing Up

Think of three things that constitute being a grown-up, and write
about them. See whether the following items apply:

What is being a grown-up?
Are you a grown-up yet?
What are some things you would like to do for yourself when
you are a grown-up?
What are some things you would like to do for your family
when you are a grown-up?
What are some things you would like to do for your relatives
when you are a grown-up?
What are some things you would like to do for your friends
when you are a grown-up?
What are some things you would like to do for your country
when you are a grown-up?
What are some of the high standards grown-ups have?

Relationship Is ...

Think of three things you love about relationships, and write about them. See whether the following items apply:

> understanding each other
> caring for each other
> noticing each other
> talking to each other
> talking each other up
> supporting each other
> being drawn to each other
> wanting to have the same lifestyle as each other
> liking each other
> dancing with each other

Movies

Think of three things you love and find appropriate to share in this class, about watching a rated G movie, and write about them. See whether the following items apply:

> favorite movies
> favorite scenes
> favorite line in a movie
> favorite music in a movie
> favorite actor or actress in a movie
> favorite outfit in a movie
> favorite behavior in a movie

Honorable Person

Think of three things that constitute an honorable person, and write about them. You can also write about anyone you know. See whether the following items apply:

> keeping a promise
> being honest
> valuing self
> dedicating yourself to a valuable cause
> not doing something in secret that you would not admit in public
> not harming
> maintaining boundaries
> not letting others step all over you
> respecting others as you respect yourself
> earning respect
> forgiving
> taking the high road by letting little things go

Love Is …

Think of three things that you love, and write about them. See whether the following items apply:

> love for family
> love for friends
> love for exercise
> love for fun
> love for country
> love for entertainment
> love for nature
> love for classmates
> love for school
> love for food
> love for respect
> love for attention

reading poetry
bringing flowers
walking with someone special
sightseeing
listening to your friends
discussing values
having lunch with someone special
entertainment

Me and My Country

Think of three things you love about your country, and write about
them. See whether the following items apply:

caring for our country, America
watching fireworks
buying American products
celebrating New Year's Day
celebrating Martin Luther King Jr. Day
celebrating George Washington's birthday
celebrating Memorial Day
celebrating Independence Day
celebrating Labor Day
celebrating Columbus Day
celebrating Veterans Day
celebrating Thanksgiving Day
celebrating Christmas Day
watching American movies
enjoying American entertainment
knowing who our president is
knowing the names of all the states, including the one you
live in
knowing all the names of the state capitals and yours too
keeping our American traditions
loving everything America has to offer
loving all the opportunities you have in America
protecting your country when you are a grown-up

loving the people in your country
loving our country because it is the best place in the world
protecting our country and the people here every day
our country is special with …
supporting your country's …
being there for our country by …
being there for your parents by …
being there for your future family and future students by …
caring for your country, America

FOR TENTH-GRADE STUDENTS

My Birthday

Think of three things about your birthday, and write about them. See whether the following items apply:

> trying a new and good thing for your birthday year
> choosing an improved lifestyle
> new age-appropriate activities
> some of the fun summer activities for you this year will be ...

I Am ...

Think of three good things about yourself that are appropriate for this class, and write about them. See whether the following items apply:

> maintaining a clean car
> keeping gas in the car
> maintaining a clean room
> doing laundry, ironing, and organizing your clothes
> listening and understanding
> your time management skills
> your reliability
> your relationship management skills
> being true to yourself
> knowing the difference between wanting something and needing something
> putting your seat belt on
> doing good
> knowing self-care
> being helpful
> maintaining a clean room
> taking care of your belongings
> your birthday gifts
> your friends
> your books
> your siblings

your home
your country

Think about three things you are grateful for, and write about them. See whether the following items apply:

your family
your country
your looks
your belongings
your habits
your friends
your neighborhood
your opportunities
your school
your classmates
your cousins
your siblings
your health
your happiness
holidays
summer vacation
your doctors
your friends' personalities
your lifestyle
your hobbies

Education is...

Think about three things that you agree with or know about education and write about them. See whether the following items apply:

It is easier to become a Doctor than to become a millionaire
It is easier to make money, when you are a Doctor

Education helps become more knowledgeable
Education helps boost self-esteem
Education is fun, if you are interested in it
Education is a brain exercise
Education helps solve problems easier
Education can help earn respect
Education makes it easier to buy the things you want
Education can help you find a more stable job
Education can help you have a more stable lifestyle
Education can help you have your own business
Education is a prestige
Once you become a Doctor, you will be a Doctor for the rest of your life
Education does not make you boring
Education can give you more than what money can
With education you can have money
With education you can satisfy your scientific interests
Education can make you a well-rounded person
With education you can have a stable job by the time you are 25 years old
To become educated all you have to do is pick a subject and commit
Many people can help you become educated
Education has a clear path
With education you may never become homeless
You can be educated as well as an entrepreneur
You can be educated as well as a millionaire
Education can open many doors for you
It is very easy to become educated if you have a favorite subject
Your favorite subject in school is...
Your feelings about educated people are

Think of three things that make you feel smart and/or strong, and write about them. See whether the following items apply:

> getting good grades
> learning new words
> choosing a better vocabulary
> doing homework
> finishing homework
> exercising
> when friends call
> when you feel older
> spending time with friends
> talking to friends
> playing outdoors
> when your parents say you did a good job
> when it's your birthday
> thinking about things you have done
> putting the dishes in the sink
> getting attention from the opposite gender
> exercising for your health
> investing your time in your family
> having a good nutrition intake
> maintaining good friends
> upholding your confidence for being a good person
> choosing your behaviors wisely

Work

Think of three good things about work, and write about them. See whether the following items apply:

> favorite work
> favorite pay
> friendly colleagues compared to friendly classmates and other friends

rules at work
obedience for work
compliance to work ethics
friendly boss
friendly you
purpose of your work
contribution to society with your work
having a business
providing earth-friendly services, etc.

My Culture ...

Think of three values of our culture, and write about them. See whether the following items apply:

cultural values
cultural rituals
movies
music
food
presidents
other key figures
entertainers
talk show hosts
radio hosts
compare old movies to new movies
country songs
modern songs
cartoons
community fun and family activities
sporting events
Olympics
stadiums
economy
hot-air balloon festivals
film events, red-carpet awards
festivals

tourists and tourist attractions
structures and establishments
botanical gardens and arboretums
buildings and gardens
Renaissance fairs
fun college programs and courses
respected higher degrees
museums
comedy and humor
TV shows
camping
magazines
newspapers
new books and best novels compared to of best books and
best novels of the twentieth century
valued education

I Am a Good Person for My Family

Think of three good things that you and your family do for one
another, and write about them. See whether the following items
apply:

family as part of the community you live in
some of the things your parents do for your family
some of the things you will do for your children when you
are a parent
being grateful
having loving parents
being loving children
having caring parents
doing the laundry, ironing, and organizing your clothes
having a warm bed
having shoes that fit
washing your dishes
cooking dinner
having food

having clothes
having a roof over your head
others playing sports with you
buying gifts
making your bed
cleaning the table after dinner
putting clothes and shoes where they are supposed to be
showing respect to the elderly

Self-Control Is When I Am …

Think of three things you have self-control in, and write about them.
See whether the following items apply:

not harming yourself
not harming others
using your words and not getting into a fight
using your words and not screaming
listening to the teacher during class
exercising
dressing appropriately
keeping your cell phone on mute and controlling your phone
(instead of your phone controlling you)
not eating too many holiday candies
putting away your shoes and clothes
not interrupting
understanding that no means no

I Am Responsible When I Am …

Think of three responsibilities you take, and write about them. See
whether the following items apply:

doing your homework in a timely manner
eating healthy food
cleaning the table

putting your shoes in the closet

not losing things

I Am Caring When I Am ...

Think of three things that you care about that make you feel like a caring person, and write about them. See whether the following items apply:

> helping friends
> helping around the house
> helping my siblings
> feed the birds
> ask about others' well-being
> empathizing (not sympathizing) with people you like or love
> complimenting someone
> handling others' belongings appropriately
> driving safely
> doing something good for my country
> when you do something for your country

Being a Hero Is When ...

Think of three good things you do that make you feel like a hero, and write about them. See whether the following items apply:

> knowing honor
> knowing respect
> knowing discipline
> knowing values
> being friendly
> ability to get along with people without causing problems
> being able to express yourself without inappropriate words
> appreciating values
> ice-skating
> hiking

acing your schoolwork
being able to express yourself without inappropriate words
being on time to school
being responsible for yourself
not forgetting to have fun
protecting your family name by saying nice things about
your family
emotional and/or physical support
keeping high standards, especially the ones you appreciate
in others
promoting good behavior
knowing your priorities
knowing the cost and benefits of your actions
knowing what's good for you

The Support System in My Life ...

Think of three socializing activities you like, and write about them.
See whether the following items apply:

socializing with your mother
socializing with your father
socializing with your sister
socializing with your brother
socializing with your aunts
socializing with your uncles
socializing with your cousins
socializing with your friends
socializing with your friends' families
socializing with new and old neighbors
socializing with your relatives
socializing with your family friends
socializing with your friends at school
socializing with your teachers
socializing with your mother's friends
socializing with your mother's friends' children
socializing with your father's friends

socializing with your father's friends' children
socializing a good therapist you love
socializing with a good mentor
when friends are there for you
when your family is there for you
singing together at the dinner table
dancing together in family gatherings
sharing hopes and dreams with each other

When I Am Having Fun and It Is Healthy ...

Think of three healthy, fun activities you love that are also appropriate for this class, and write about them. See whether the following items apply:

playing sports
camping
playing board games
watching games
dancing
making friends
petting an animal
vacationing with family
talking to friends
swimming
meeting with relatives
traveling throughout the United States

Girls Are Similar to and Different from Boys ...

Think of three ways that boys and girls are similar or different, and write about them. See whether the following items apply:

choice of clothing
shoes
interests

hobbies
games
dream job
food
exercise habits
sport activities
hair color
eye color
cars they drive
last names
signing abilities
dancing abilities
abilities to do school work
abilities to put their shoes in their proper place
abilities for washing the dishes
boys are supportive when …
girls are supportive when …
valuable girl behaviors
valuable boy behaviors
some of the things guys do that make others feel valuable
some of the things girls do that make others feel valuable
some of the things that make girls special
some of the things that make boys special
attention, goals, self-presentations, self-care, attire, etc.

Growing Up

Think of three things that constitute being a grown-up, and write about them. See whether the following items apply:

What is being a grown-up?
Are you a grown-up yet?
What are some things you would like to do for yourself when you are a grown-up?
What are some things you would like to do for your family when you are a grown-up?

What are some things you would like to do for your relatives when you are a grown-up?

What are some things you would like to do for your friends when you are a grown-up?

What are some things you would like to do for your country when you are a grown-up?

What are some of the high standards grown-ups have?

Relationship Is …

Think of three things you love about relationships, and write about them. See whether the following items apply:

understanding each other
caring for each other
noticing each other
talking to each other
talking each other up
supporting each other
being drawn to each other
wanting to have the same lifestyle as each other
liking each other
dancing with each other

Movies

Think of three things you love and find appropriate to share in this class, about watching a rated G movie, and write about them. See whether the following items apply:

favorite movies
favorite scenes
favorite line in a movie
favorite music in a movie
favorite actor or actress in a movie
favorite outfit in a movie

favorite behavior in a movie

Honorable Person

Think of three things you love about an honorable person, and write about them. See whether the following items apply:

keeping a promise
being honest
valuing self
dedicating yourself to a valuable cause
not doing something in secret that you would not admit in public
not harming
maintaining boundaries
not letting others step all over you
respecting others as you respect yourself
earning respect
forgiving
taking the high road by letting little things go

Love Is …

Think of three good things you love, and write about them. See whether the following items apply:

love for family
love for friends
love for exercise
love for fun
love for country
love for entertainment
love for nature
love for classmates
love for school
love for food

love for respect
love for attention
reading poetry
bringing flowers
walking with someone special
sightseeing
listening
expressing values
having lunch with …
entertainment

Me and My Country

Think of three things you love about your country, and write about them. See whether the following items apply:

caring for our country, America
watching fireworks
buying American products
celebrating New Year's Day
celebrating Martin Luther King Jr. Day
celebrating George Washington's birthday
celebrating Memorial Day
celebrating Independence Day
celebrating Labor Day
celebrating Columbus Day
celebrating Veterans Day
celebrating Thanksgiving Day
celebrating Christmas Day
watching American movies
enjoying American entertainment
knowing who our president is
knowing the names of all the states, including the one you live in
knowing all the names of the state capitals and yours too
keeping our American traditions
loving everything America has to offer

loving all the opportunities you have in America
protecting your country when you are a grown-up
loving the people in your country
loving your country as the best place in the world
protecting your country and the people here every day
your country is special because of …
supporting your country's …
being there for your country by …
being there for your parents by …
being there for your future family and future students by …
caring for your country, America
being there for your future family and children by caring for
your country, America
your country includes your family, your friends, your
friends' families, your relatives, and your potential families

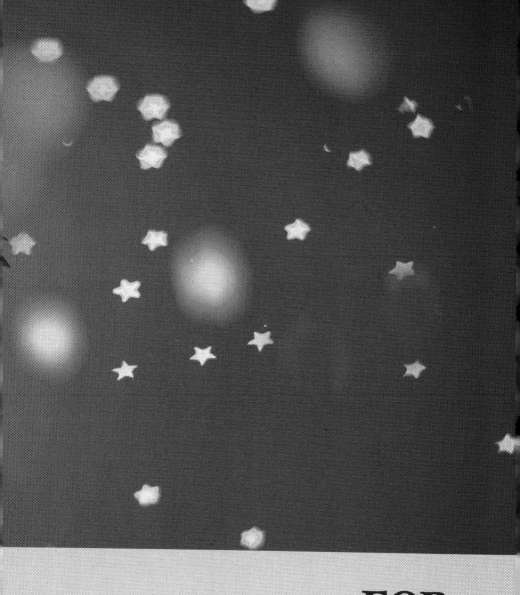

FOR ELEVENTH-GRADE STUDENTS

My Birthday

Think of three things about your birthday, and write about them. See whether the following items apply:

> trying a new and good thing for my birthday year
> choosing an improved lifestyle
> new age-appropriate activities
> some of the fun summer activities for you this year will be …

I Am …

Think of three good things about yourself that are appropriate for this class, and write about them. See whether the following items apply:

> maintaining a clean car
> keeping gas in the car
> maintaining a clean room
> doing laundry and ironing
> listening and understanding family
> listening and understanding friends
> your time management skills
> your reliability
> your relationship management skills
> being true to yourself
> knowing the difference between wanting something and needing something
> putting your seat belt on
> doing good
> being helpful
> your room is clean
> taking care of your belongings
> your birthday gifts
> your friends
> your books
> your siblings

your home
your country

Think about three things you are grateful for, and write about them.
See whether the following items apply:

your family
your country
your looks
your belongings
your habits
your friends
your neighborhood
your opportunities
your school
your classmates
your cousins
your siblings
your health
your happiness
holidays
summer vacation
your doctors
your friends' personalities
your lifestyle
your hobbies
your standards
your values

Education is…

Think about three things that you agree with or know about education and write about them. See whether the following items apply:

It is easier to become a Doctor than to become a millionaire
It is easier to make money, when you are a Doctor
Education helps become more knowledgeable
Education helps boost self-esteem
Education is fun, if you are interested in it
Education is a brain exercise
Education helps solve problems easier
Education can help earn respect
Education makes it easier to buy the things you want
Education can help you find a more stable job
Education can help you have a more stable lifestyle
Education can help you have your own business
Education is a prestige
Once you become a Doctor, you will be a Doctor for the rest of your life
Education does not make you boring
Education can give you more than what money can
With education you can have money
With education you can satisfy your scientific interests
Education can make you a well-rounded person
With education you can have a stable job by the time you are 25 years old
To become educated all you have to do is pick a subject and commit
Many people can help you become educated
Education has a clear path
With education you may never become homeless
You can be educated as well as an entrepreneur
You can be educated as well as a millionaire
Education can open many doors for you
It is very easy to become educated if you have a favorite subject

Your favorite subject in school is...
Your feelings about educated people are

I Feel Smart and/or Strong When I Am ...

Think of three things that make you feel smart and/or strong, and write about them. See whether the following items apply:

getting good grades
learning new words
choosing a better vocabulary
doing homework
finishing homework
exercising
when friends call
when you feel older
spending time with friends
talking to friends
playing outdoors
when your parents say you did a good job
when it's your birthday
thinking about things you have done
putting your dishes in the sink
getting attention from the opposite gender
when you exercise for your health
when you invest your time in your family
when you have a good nutrition intake
maintaining good friends
upholding your confidence for being a good person
choosing your behaviors

Work

Think of three good things about your work, and write about them. See whether the following items apply:

favorite work
favorite pay
friendly colleagues compared to friendly classmates and
other friends
rules at work
obedience for work
compliance to work ethics
friendly boss
friendly you
purpose of your work
contribution to society with your work
having a business
providing earth-friendly services, etc.

My Culture ...

Think of three good things about your culture, and write about
them. See whether the following items apply:

cultural values
cultural rituals
movies
music
food
presidents and other key figures
entertainers
talk shows
radio shows
compare old movies to new movies
country songs
modern songs
cartoons
community fun and family activities
sporting events
Olympics
stadiums
economy

hot-air balloon festivals
film events, red-carpet awards
festivals
tourists and tourist attractions
structures and establishments
botanical gardens and arboretums
buildings and gardens
Renaissance fairs
fun college programs and courses
respected higher degrees
museums
comedy and humor
TV shows
camping
magazines
newspapers
new books and the best novels compared to the best books
and novels of the twentieth century
valued education

I Am a Good Person for My Family

Think of three good things that you and your family do for one another, and write about them. See whether the following items apply:

family as part of your community you live in
some of the things your parents do for your family
some of the things you will do for your children when you
are a parent
being grateful
having loving parents
having caring parents
doing the laundry, ironing, and organizing clothes
having a warm bed
having shoes that fit
washing your dishes

cooking dinner
having food
having clothes
having a roof over your head
others playing sports with you
buying gifts
making your bed
cleaning the table after dinner
putting your clothes and shoes where they are supposed
to be
showing respect to the elderly

Self-Control Is When I Am ...

Think of three things you have self-control in, and write about them.
See whether the following items apply:

not harming yourself
not harming others
using your words and not getting into a fight
using your words and not screaming
exercising
dressing up appropriately
keeping your cell phone on mute and controlling your phone
(instead of your phone controlling you)
not eating too many holiday candies
putting away your shoes and clothes
not interrupting
not talking during class
understanding that no mean no

I Am Responsible When I Am ...

Think of three responsibilities you have, and write about them. See
whether the following items apply:

doing your homework in a timely manner
eating healthy food
cleaning the table
putting your shoes in the closet
not losing things

I Am Caring When I Am

Think of three things that you care about that make you feel like a caring person, and write about them. See whether the following items apply:

helping friends
helping around the house
helping my siblings
feed the birds
ask about others' well-being
empathizing (not sympathizing) with people you like or love
complimenting someone
handling others' belongings appropriately
driving safely
contributing to a good cause
doing something good for my country
when you do something for your country

Being a Hero Is When I Am ...

Think of three things that make you feel like a hero, and write about them. See whether the following items apply:

knowing honor
knowing respect
knowing discipline
knowing values
being friendly
buying made-in-the-USA products

driving responsibly

not paying too much for car insurance

ability to get along with other people without causing problems

appreciating values

riding a bike

ice-skating

acing your schoolwork

being able to express yourself without inappropriate words

being on time to school

being responsible for yourself

not forgetting to have fun

protecting your family name by saying nice things about your family

emotional and/or physical support

keeping high standards especially the ones you appreciate in others

knowing the cost and benefits for your actions

knowing what's good for you

showing gratitude to your family

maintaining a good reputation within the family

maintaining a good reputation in school

maintaining a good reputation with friends

maintaining a good reputation with relatives

maintaining a good reputation at workplace

The Support System in My Life ...

Think of three socializing activities you like, and write about them. See whether the following items apply:

socializing with your mother
socializing with your father
socializing with your sister
socializing with your brother
socializing with your aunts
socializing with your uncles

socializing with your cousins
socializing with your friends
socializing with your friends' families
socializing with new and old neighbors
socializing with your relatives
socializing with your family friends
socializing with your friends at school
socializing with your teachers
socializing with your mother's friends
socializing with your mother's friends' children
socializing with your father's friends
socializing with your father's friends' children
socializing with a good therapist you love
socializing with a good mentor
when your friends are there for you
when your family is there for you
singing together at the dinner table
dancing together at family gatherings
sharing hopes and dreams with each other, etc.

When I Am Having Fun and It Is Healthy ...

Think of three healthy, fun activities you love that are also appropriate for this class, and write about them. See whether the following items apply:

playing sports
camping
playing board games
watching games
dancing
making friends
petting an animal
vacationing with family
talking to friends
swimming
meeting with relatives

traveling throughout the United States

Girls Are Similar to and Different from Boys …

Think of three ways that boys and girls are similar or different, and write about them. See whether the following items apply:

choice of clothing
shoes
interests
hobbies
games
dream job
food
exercise habits
sport activities
hair color
eye color
cars they drive
last names
signing abilities
dancing abilities
abilities to do school work
abilities to put their shoes in their proper place
abilities for washing the dishes
boys are supportive when …
girls are supportive when …
valuable girl behaviors
valuable boy behaviors
some of the things guys do that make others feel valuable
some of the things girls do that make others feel valuable
some of the things that make girls special
some of the things that make boys special
attention, goals, self-presentations, self-care, attire, etc.

Growing Up

Think of three things that constitute being a grown-up, and write about them. See whether the following items apply:

> What is being a grown-up?
> Are you a grown-up yet?
> What are some things you would like to do for yourself when you are a grown-up?
> What are some things you would like to do for your family when you are a grown-up?
> What are some things you would like to do for your relatives when you are a grown-up?
> What are some things you would like to do for your friends when you are a grown-up?
> What are some things you would like to do for your country when you are a grown-up?
> What are some of the high standards grown-ups have?

Relationship Is ...

Think of three things you love about relationships, and write about them. See whether the following items apply:

> understanding each other
> caring for each other
> noticing each other
> talking to each other
> talking each other up
> supporting each other
> being drawn to each other
> wanting to have the same lifestyle as each other
> liking each other
> dancing with each other

Movies

Think of three things you love and find appropriate to share in this class, about watching a rated G movie, and write about them. See whether the following items apply:

favorite movies
favorite scenes
favorite line in a movie
favorite music in a movie
favorite actor or actress in a movie
favorite outfit in a movie
favorite behavior in a movie

Honorable Person

Think of three things that constitute an honorable person, and write about them. You can also write about anyone you know. See whether the following items apply:

keeping a promise
being honest
valuing self
valuing others
dedicating yourself to a valuable cause
not doing something in secret that you would not admit in public
not harming others
maintaining boundaries
not letting others step all over you
respecting others as you respect yourself
earning respect
forgiving
taking the high road by letting little things go

Love Is …

Think of three good things you love, and write about them. See whether the following items apply:

> love for family
> love for friends
> love for exercise
> love for fun
> love for country
> love for entertainment
> love for nature
> love for classmates
> love for school
> love for food
> love for respect
> love for attention
> reading poetry
> bringing flowers
> walking with someone special
> sightseeing
> listening to a friend
> expressing values
> having lunch with …
> entertainment

Me and My Country

Think of three things you love about your country, and write about them. See whether the following items apply:

> caring for our country, America
> watching fireworks
> buying American products
> celebrating New Year's Day
> celebrating Martin Luther King Jr. Day
> celebrating George Washington's birthday

celebrating Memorial Day
celebrating Independence Day
celebrating Labor Day
celebrating Columbus Day
celebrating Veterans Day
celebrating Thanksgiving Day
celebrating Christmas Day
watching American movies
enjoying American entertainment
knowing who our president is
knowing the names of all the states, including the one you
live in
knowing all the names of the state capitals and yours too
keeping our American traditions
loving everything America has to offer
loving all the opportunities you have in America
protecting your country when you are a grown-up
loving the people in your country
loving our country for being the best place in the world
protecting our country and the people here every day
our country is special because of …
supporting your country's …
being there for your country by …
being there for your parents by …
being there for your future family and future students by …
caring for your country, America
being there for your future family and children by caring for
your country, America
your country includes your family, your friends, your
friends' families, your relatives, and your potential families

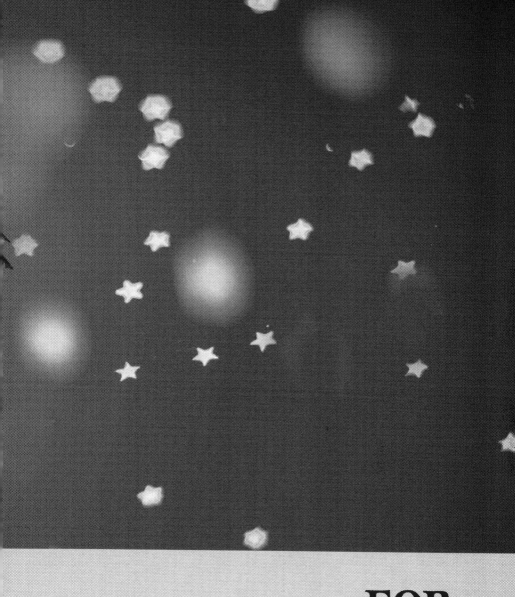

FOR
TWELFTH-GRADE
STUDENTS

My Birthday

Think of three things about your birthday, and write about them. See whether the following items apply:

> trying new and good things for your birthday year
> choosing an improved lifestyle
> choosing new, age-appropriate activities
> some of the fun summer activities for you this year will be ...

I Am ...

Think of three good things about yourself that are appropriate for this class, and write about them. See whether the following items apply:

> maintaining a clean car
> keeping gas in your car
> maintaining a clean room
> doing laundry, ironing, and organizing the clothes
> listening and understanding your family
> listening and understanding your friends
> your time management skills
> your reliability
> your relationship management skills
> being true to yourself
> knowing the difference between wanting something and needing something
> putting your seat belt on
> doing good for others
> being helpful
> your room is clean
> taking care of your belongings
> your birthday gifts
> your friends
> your books
> your siblings

your home
your country

I Am Grateful for …

Think about three things you are grateful for, and write about them. See whether the following items apply:

your family
your country
your looks
your belongings
your habits
your friends
your neighborhood
your opportunities
your school
your classmates
your cousins
your siblings
your health
your happiness
holidays
summer vacation
your doctors
your friends' personalities
your lifestyle
your hobbies
your standards
your social skills
your abilities
your values

Education is...

Think about three things that you agree with or know about education and write about them. See whether the following items apply:

It is easier to become a Doctor than to become a millionaire
It is easier to make money, when you are a Doctor
Education helps become more knowledgeable
Education helps boost self-esteem
Education is fun, if you are interested in it
Education is a brain exercise
Education helps solve problems easier
Education can help earn respect
Education makes it easier to buy the things you want
Education can help you find a more stable job
Education can help you have a more stable lifestyle
Education can help you have your own business
Education is a prestige
Once you become a Doctor, you will be a Doctor for the rest of your life
Education does not make you boring
Education can give you more than what money can
With education you can have money
With education you can satisfy your scientific interests
Education can make you a well-rounded person
With education you can have a stable job by the time you are 25 years old
To become educated all you have to do is pick a subject and commit
Many people can help you become educated
Education has a clear path
With education you may never become homeless
You can be educated as well as an entrepreneur
You can be educated as well as a millionaire
Education can open many doors for you
It is very easy to become educated if you have a favorite subject

Your favorite subject in school is…
Your feelings about educated people are

I Feel Smart and/or Strong When I Am …

Think of three things that make you feel smart and/or strong, and write about them. See whether the following items apply:

getting good grades
learning new words
choosing a better vocabulary
doing your homework
finishing your homework
exercising
when friends call
when I feel older
spending time with friends
talking to friends
playing outdoors
when your parents say you did a good job
when it's your birthday
thinking about things you have done
putting your dishes in the sink
getting attention from the opposite gender
exercising for your health
investing your time in your family
getting a good nutritional intake
maintaining good friends
upholding your confidence for being a good person
choosing your behaviors

Work

Think of three good things about working, and write about them. See whether the following items apply:

> favorite work
> favorite pay
> friendly colleagues compared to friendly classmates and other friends
> rules at work
> obedience for work
> compliance to work ethics
> friendly boss
> friendly you
> purpose of your work
> your contribution to society with your work
> having a business
> providing earth-friendly services

My Culture ...

Think of three things you love about our culture, and write about them. See whether the following items apply:

> cultural values
> cultural rituals
> movies
> music
> food
> presidents
> other key figures
> entertainers
> talk show hosts
> radio hosts
> compare old movies to new movies
> country songs
> modern songs

cartoons
community fun and family activities
sporting events
Olympics
stadiums
economy
hot-air balloon festivals
film events, red–carpet awards
festivals
tourists and tourist attractions
structures and establishments
botanical gardens and arboretums
buildings and gardens
Renaissance fairs
fun college programs and courses
respected higher degrees
museums
comedy and humor
TV shows
camping
magazines
newspapers
new books and best novels compared to best books and best
novels of the twentieth century
a valued education

I Am a Good Person for My Family

Ask students whether they know the things their families do for
them, and ask them to write about the following:

> your family as part of your community you live in
> some of the things your parents do for your family
> some of the things you will do for your children when you
> are a parent
> being grateful
> having loving parents

being loving children
having caring parents
doing laundry, ironing, and organizing your clothes
having a warm bed
having shoes that fit
washing your dishes
having food
cooking dinner
having clothes
the roof over your head
others playing sports with you
buying gifts
making your bed
cleaning the table
doing your homework
putting clothes and shoes where they are supposed to be
showing respect to the elderly

Self-Control Is When I Am ...

Think of three things you have self-control in, and write about them.
See whether the following items apply:

not harming yourself
not harming others
using your words and not getting into a fight
using your words and not screaming
listening to the teacher instead of making noise in the classroom
exercising
dressing appropriately
keeping your cell phone on mute and controlling your phone (instead of your phone controlling you)
not eating too many holiday candies
putting away your clothes and shoes
not interrupting
understanding that no means no

I Am Responsible When I Am …

Think of three good things you take responsibility for, and write about them. See whether the following items apply:

> doing your homework in a timely manner
> eating healthy food
> cleaning the table
> putting your clothes and shoes in the closet
> not losing things

I Am Caring When I Am …

Think of three things that you care about, which makes you feel like a caring person, and write about them. See whether the following items apply:

> helping friends
> helping around the house
> helping my siblings
> feed the birds
> ask about others' well–beings
> empathizing (not sympathizing) with people you like or love
> complimenting someone
> handling others' belongings appropriately
> driving safely
> when you do something for your country

Being a Hero Is When I Am …

Think of three good things you do that make you feel like a hero, that are also appropriate for this class, and write about them. See whether the following items apply:

> buying made-in-the-USA products
> knowing honor

knowing respect
knowing discipline
knowing values
being friendly
driving responsibly and safely
not paying too much for car insurance
having the ability to get along with other people without causing problems
appreciating values
riding a bike
ice-skating
acing your schoolwork
being able to express yourself without inappropriate words
being on time to school
being responsible for yourself
not forgetting to have fun
protecting your family name by saying nice things about them
emotional and/or physical support
keeping high standards especially the ones you appreciate in others
knowing the cost and benefits for your actions
showing gratitude to your family
maintaining a good reputation within your family
maintaining a good reputation in your school
maintaining a good reputation with your friends
maintaining a good reputation with your relatives
maintaining a good reputation at your workplace

The Support System in My Life ...

Think of three socializing activities you like, and write about them. See whether the following items apply:

socializing with your mother
socializing with your father
socializing with your sister

socializing with your brother
socializing with your aunts
socializing with your uncles
socializing with your cousins
socializing with your friends
socializing with your friends' families
socializing with new and old neighbors
socializing with your relatives
socializing with your family friends
socializing with your friends at school
socializing with your teachers
socializing with your mother's friends
socializing with your mother's friends' children
socializing with your father's friends
socializing with your father's friends' children
socializing with a good therapist you love
socializing with a good mentor
when your friends are there for you
when your family is there for you
singing together at the dinner table
dancing together at family gatherings
sharing hopes and dreams with each other

When I Am Having Fun and It Is Healthy ...

Think of three healthy, fun activities you love that are also appropriate for this class, and write about them. See whether the following items apply:

playing sports
camping
playing board games
watching games
dancing
making friends
petting an animal
vacationing with family

talking to friends
swimming
meeting with relatives
traveling throughout the United States

Girls Are Similar to and Different from Boys ...

Think of three ways that boys and girls are similar or different, and write about them. See whether the following items apply:

choice of clothing
shoes
interests
hobbies
games
dream job
food
exercise habits
sport activities
hair color
eye color
cars they drive
last names
signing abilities
dancing abilities
abilities to do school work
abilities to put the shoes in their places
abilities for washing the dishes
boys are supportive when ...
girls are supportive when ...
valuable girl behaviors
valuable boy behaviors
some of the things guys do that make others feel valuable
some of the things girls do that make others feel valuable
some of the things that make girls special
some of the things that make boys special
attention, goals, self-presentation, self-care, attire, etc.

Growing Up

Think of three things that constitute being a grown-up, and write about them. See whether the following items apply:

> What is being a grown-up?
> Are you a grown-up yet?
> What are some things you would like to do for yourself when you are a grown-up?
> What are some things you would like to do for your family when you are a grown-up?
> What are some things you would like to do for your relatives when you are a grown-up?
> What are some things you would like to do for your friends when you are a grown-up?
> What are some things you would like to do for your country when you are a grown-up?
> What are some of the high standards grown-ups have?

Relationship Is …

Think of three things you love about relationships, and write about them. See whether the following items apply:

> understanding each other
> caring for each other
> noticing each other
> talking to each other
> talking each other up
> supporting each other
> being drawn to each other
> wanting to have the same lifestyle as each other
> liking each other
> dancing with each other

Movies

Think of three things you love and find appropriate to share in this class, about watching a rated G movie, and write about them. See whether the following items apply:

favorite movies
favorite scenes
favorite line in a movie
favorite music in a movie
favorite actor or actress in a movie
favorite outfit in a movie
favorite behavior in a movie

Honorable Person

Think of three things that constitute an honorable person, and write about them. You can also write about anyone you know. See whether the following items apply:

keeping a promise
being honest
valuing self
valuing others
dedicating yourself to a valuable cause
not doing something in secret that you would not admit in public
not harming others
maintaining boundaries
not letting others step all over you
respecting others as you respect yourself
earning respect
forgiving
taking the high road by letting little things go
standing up for yourself
standing up for your friends

standing up for your family
standing up for your country

Love Is …

Think of three things you love, and write about them. See whether the following items apply:

love for family
love for friends
love for exercise
love for fun
love for country
love for entertainment
love for nature
love for school
love for classmates
love for food
love for respect
love for attention
reading poetry
bringing flowers
walking with someone special
sightseeing
listening to a friend
discussing values
having lunch with friends
entertainment

Me and My Country

Think of three things you love about your country, and write about them. See whether the following items apply:

caring for our country, America
watching fireworks

buying American products
celebrating New Year's Day
celebrating Martin Luther King Jr. Day
celebrating George Washington's birthday
celebrating Memorial Day
celebrating Independence Day
celebrating Labor Day
celebrating Columbus Day
celebrating Veterans Day
celebrating Thanksgiving Day
celebrating Christmas Day
watching American movies
enjoying American entertainment
knowing who our president is
knowing the names of all the states, including the one you
live in
knowing all the names of the state capitals and yours too
keeping our American traditions
loving everything America has to offer
loving all the opportunities you have in America
protecting your country when you are a grown-up
loving the people in your country
loving your country because it is the best place in the world
protecting your country and the people here every day
your country is special because of …
supporting your country's …
being there for your country by …
being there for your parents by …
being there for your future family and future students by …
caring for your country, America
being there for your future family and children by caring for
your country, America
your country includes your family, your friends, your
friends' families, your relatives, and your potential families

Printed in the United States
By Bookmasters